What Mary Means to Christians

AN ANCIENT TRADITION EXPLAINED

REVEREND PETER M. J.
STRAVINSKAS

Paulist Press
New York / Mahwah, NJ

Cover image: Copyright by Zvonimir Atletic / Shutterstock.com
Cover design by Sharyn Banks
Book design by Lynn Else

Library of Congress Cataloging-in-Publication Data

Stravinskas, Peter M. J.
    What Mary means to Christians : an ancient tradition explained / Peter M. J. Stravinskas.
        p. cm.
    Includes bibliographical references (p.   ).
    ISBN 978-0-8091-4744-1 (alk. paper) 1. Mary, Blessed Virgin, Saint. I. Title.
    BT603.S77 2012
    232.91—dc23

                                                                    2011033018

Published by Paulist Press
997 Macarthur Boulevard
Mahwah, New Jersey 07430

www.paulistpress.com

Printed and bound in the
United States of America

CONTENTS

Contents

Contents

INTRODUCTION

"Do Catholics worship Mary and the other saints?"

Catholics are often insulted by this question and frequently refuse to answer it for that reason alone. A nonresponse, however, is not helpful for a variety of reasons, not least of which is that it is an extremely important question—the answer to which determines whether one is a Christian.

The relationship between Catholics and Mary mystifies many non-Catholic Christians, and Catholics are equally mystified by their strange silence about her—a silence that is awkward and uncomfortable, a silence that is usually broken only once a year at Christmastime because ancient carols force believers to acknowledge and sing of the Virgin who became the Mother of the Messiah. Of course, not all non-Catholic Christians fall into this category: Eastern Orthodox devotion to the Mother of God is very strong, many Anglicans and Lutherans share our convictions about the Blessed Virgin, and one of the best books on the Rosary was written by a Methodist minister.[1] By and large, though, Protestants have not followed the example of John the Beloved Disciple by making room in their homes for the Mother of Our Lord (John 19:27). It may also surprise some readers to learn that Islam holds Our Lady in great reverence; in fact, there are more references to Mary in the Koran than in the New Testament!

Catholics need to become better spokespersons for Marian devotion, both in their articulation of it and in their understanding of its scriptural basis. In many circumstances, an honest dialogue brings to light that the problem of many non-Catholics with Mary is not so much Mary herself as the way she is presented. Such people need to be challenged forthrightly and charitably to think

1

about Mary and to reflect on their usual silence (and even hostility) in her regard. Our goal should not be to rouse their sensibilities to the heights of Marian devotion, but to raise their consciousness to an appreciation of the role of the Blessed Virgin in her Son's work of salvation.

The teaching of the Scriptures and the Church is clear: Jesus Christ is the sole Mediator between God and man (1 Tim 2:5). No other person in Heaven or on Earth can take His place. The role of every saint is to lead the believer to Christ. This subordinate form of mediation derives its meaning and effectiveness from the Lord Himself and is not something the saints possess on their own.

Where, then, does Mary fit into the picture?

Catholics look on Mary, above all, as a model and guide. By her "yes" to the will of the Father at the Annunciation, Mary became the first and best Christian ever to live. Her life is a testimony to the wonderful things that can happen when the human person cooperates with the divine plan. In agreeing to be the human vessel that brought the Messiah into the world, the Blessed Mother played an essential part in Christ's salvific mission. She manifested Christian humility and obedience when she responded to God's will: "Behold, I am the handmaid of the Lord; let it be to me according to your word" (Luke 1:38). Her faith in God and her response to His will mark Mary as the first human being to accept Christ, body and soul, as she welcomed Him into her very self. The Church ever since echoes the words of Mary's kinswoman Elizabeth, as she proclaimed: "And blessed is she who believed that there would be a fulfillment of what was spoken to her from the Lord" (Luke 1:45).

Let me state at the outset what this book is *not*. It is not intended to be a comprehensive Mariological treatise; nor is it exclusively devotional in character. I have tried to produce a work that will serve a number of purposes for the average well-educated and devout Catholic. And so, we shall be looking at the figure of Our Lady, first of all, through the Sacred Scriptures, but also from doctrinal and liturgical perspectives. As already mentioned, there is an apologetical dimension to our considerations, that is, a conscious effort to present Marian doctrine and devotion in a manner that is biblically rooted and theologically sound, and thus comprehensible to those for whom this is often seen as dangerous territory—which likewise makes this work a contribution to ecumenical dialogue, for genuine dialogue can only occur when misunderstandings are cleared away.

Each meditation closes with some thoughts from a great English convert of the nineteenth century, John Henry Cardinal Newman. Why Newman, one might ask? Several reasons suggest themselves. First of all, the case has been made by many that Blessed Cardinal Newman may well have been the most important theologian writing in English in the past several centuries. Indeed, every pope of the twentieth century envisioned him a Doctor of the Church, should he be canonized, which leads to the second point. While I was working on this text, I was inspired by Newman's then-pending beatification, the penultimate step to canonization. Most significant, that ceremony was presided over by Pope Benedict himself (despite his personal policy to delegate beatifications to lower levels of the hierarchy) because of his belief that Newman has such a universal value. Third, as a Protestant, Newman was thoroughly hostage to what we can call "Marian neuralgia." One of the first results of his intensive study of the Fathers of the Church, however, was being cured of this neuralgia, so that he became— even while still a Protestant—a Marian apologist. The excerpts from his writings on Our Lady are broad-ranging: from sermons, to letters, to treatises, written over decades, both before and after his entrance into full communion with the Catholic Church. A word of warning is in order, namely, that Newman is not a G. K. Chesterton or a Fulton J. Sheen, known for short, pithy, one-liners. He can be dense, but probing his writing is well worth the effort to experience the depth, tenderness, and beauty of his thoughts on the Mother of God.

At Newman's Mass of Beatification in Birmingham, England, celebrated on September 19, 2010, the Holy Father led into his Sunday Angelus address with the following reflection on Blessed John Henry's Mariology:

> When Blessed John Henry Newman came to live in Birmingham, he gave the name "Maryvale" to his first home here. The Oratory that he founded is dedicated to the Immaculate Conception of the Blessed Virgin. And the Catholic University of Ireland he placed under the patronage of Mary, Sedes Sapientiae. In so many ways, he lived his priestly ministry in a spirit of filial devotion to the Mother of God. Meditating upon her role in the unfolding of God's plan for our salvation, he was moved to exclaim: "Who can estimate the holiness and perfection of her, who was chosen to be the Mother of Christ? What must have been her gifts, who was chosen to be the only near earthly relative of the Son of God, the only one whom He was bound by nature to revere and look up to; the one appointed to train and educate Him, to instruct Him day by day, as He grew in wisdom and in stature?" (Parochial and Plain Sermons, ii, 131–32). It is on account of those abundant gifts of grace that we honor her, and it is on account of that intimacy with her divine Son that we naturally seek her intercession for our own needs and the needs of the whole world. In the words of the Angelus, we turn now to our Blessed Mother and commend to her the intentions that we hold in our hearts.

Introduction

I complete this labor of love on the liturgical memorial of the Immaculate Heart of Mary, having as my motive an effort to enable others, in the profound and poetic words of Pope John Paul II, "to contemplate the face of Christ in union with, and at the school of, his Most Holy Mother" (*Rosarium Virginis Mariae*, n. 3).

The Life of Mary

THE IMMACULATE CONCEPTION

The doctrine of the Immaculate Conception of Mary holds that no stain of Adam's sin touched the Blessed Virgin. That says something about Mary, of course, but it points in two other directions as well. First, it says that this privilege accorded to her was in virtue of her role as Mother of the Messiah, in order to make her a worthy dwelling for Him. Second, it is a reminder that through Christ's redeeming death and resurrection, all believers have the stain of original sin washed from their souls in the waters of Baptism. Some Christians become nervous with this doctrine because they think it removes Mary from the rest of humanity and raises her to the level of a goddess. They point to the fact that in her *Magnificat*, Mary sings of "God my Savior" (Luke 1:47), thus implicitly acknowledging her own need for redemption. Catholic theology explains this by asserting that Mary was indeed redeemed by God through "prevenient grace." This term of scholastic theology simply means that God spared Mary from sin, crediting to her in advance the benefits of her Son's redemptive sacrifice, so that she could sinlessly bear the sinless Son of God. It is important to remember that the concept of time is a human construct and that God lives in an eternal present; therefore, what sounds so strange to us is, in fact, not at all strange for Him. To deny this possibility is to limit the power of God.

As a talking point in ecumenical conversations, it is good to note that the Reformation principle of *sola gratia* ("grace alone") is verified in a unique way by the dogma of the Immaculate Conception: Mary is the recipient of pure, unmerited grace. To be sure, she had to respond to the overtures of divine grace, but the initiative was God's. In this dynamic between Creator and creature, we see a valuable paradigm for understanding how Almighty

God works with all of us: He offers us His all-powerful grace and awaits our cooperation. The Virgin of Nazareth is *the* model of both receptivity and response.

∞

By the Immaculate Conception of the Blessed Virgin is meant the great revealed truth that she was conceived in the womb of her mother, St. Anne, without original sin. Since the fall of Adam all mankind, his descendants, are conceived and born in sin.... But Mary never was in this state; she was by the eternal decree of God exempted from it.... It was decreed [by the Father], not that she should be cleansed from sin, but that she should, from the first moment of her being, be preserved from sin; so that the Evil One never had any part in her. Therefore, she was a child of Adam and Eve as if they had never fallen; she did not share with them their sin; she inherited the gifts and graces (and more than those) which Adam and Eve possessed in Paradise.[2]

THE BIRTH OF MARY

We know relatively little of Our Lady's origins; most of our information comes from the *Protoevangelium of St. James*, which contains many pious legends and traditions, including information about her parents and infancy. That work informs us that her parents' names were Anne and Joachim. We can imagine that every devout Jewish woman dreamed of being the mother of the Messiah, or at least of giving birth to a daughter who would be. The Church Universal commemorates Mary's birth on September 8 each year, when we are presented with Jesus' genealogy according to St. Matthew (1:1–17)— a rather strange Gospel passage, with even stranger names. Can we make some sense of it all?

St. Matthew presents us with a thoroughly Jewish Jesus, intending to show the continuity between Christianity and Judaism—indeed, the fulfillment of the latter in the former. Therefore, he pictures Jesus as the "new Moses," the Church as the "new Israel," and the Gospel as the "new Law." He does this in a variety of ways, from the five-book structure of his work to parallel the five books of the Torah, to frequent use of the number seven, to the dozens of citations of texts from the Old Testament. But the Evangelist also does something else to make this point, and does it so subtly that most readers miss it. This genealogy is a powerful proclamation of the Jewishness of Jesus, the reason for which is to announce and to demonstrate in a definitive manner that Jesus is a real son of David, from whom the long-awaited Messiah would come, according to the prophets.

To appreciate the genealogy in all its intricacy, it is important to understand, first of all, that the Jews (like most ancient peoples) had a great fascination with the symbolic value and meaning of numbers. For them, "seven" was the sign of absolute perfection, while "six" epitomized gross imperfection. No surprise, then, that the Messiah's lineage is broken into three groups of fourteen ancestors (twice the number of perfection and also the numerical value of the letters in David's name).

This genealogy is not historical in our modern understanding of the word, especially since there are many gaps in it. It does not tell us the lineage of the human race from Adam (like St. Luke's), but the lineage of the Hebrew race from Abraham, the man the Roman Canon calls "our father in faith." This list is punctuated by the most important events in Jewish history: the origins of the people, the kingship of David, the Babylonian exile, the coming of the Messiah.

This work is significant for its differences from standard Hebrew genealogies, particularly in that some women are included: Tamar, who seduced her father-in-law Judah into an incestuous union (Gen 38); Rahab, the chief prostitute of Jericho, who sheltered Joshua's spies (Josh 2); Bathsheba, the wife of Uriah, who committed adultery with David (2 Sam 11); Ruth, the wife of Boaz and daughter-in-law of Naomi, who stands as an exemplar of faithful love and devotion.

The inclusion of these women is notable for several reasons. First, the unsavory nature of most of them (and of many of the men) is a salutary reminder that all of us, and the Son of God as well, come into this world with a history. Second, the fact that three of them are not only women but also foreigners points to Jesus' mission to the Gentiles. The third reason must be understood in light of the fact that in a patriarchal society such as that of the Jews, name and property were passed on through males, not females. So the mention of these women serves as a crucial affirmation of the importance of the woman Mary, "of whom Jesus was born, who is called Christ" (Matt 1:16). It is likewise interesting to note that the genealogy is indeed Joseph's and not Mary's. The legal patrimony of Our Lord had to come through a male; however, His human origins did not come through a male, a point made eminently clear by the Evangelist: "Jacob *the father of* Joseph," but "Joseph *the husband of* Mary, of whom Jesus was born."

St. Matthew wants us to comprehend that salvation history had reached a high-water mark in the birth of Jesus; it was a brand new thing, for which Almighty God had prepared from all eternity. It was in truth the coming of Emmanuel—"God with us"—the most significant event in history. And it occurred through the agency of a woman, unaided by a man! I think it is completely accurate to say that with the advent of "God in the flesh," the status of women was unalterably changed.

First: "Let it be to me according to your word."

Then: "And the Word became flesh."

Each and every time we imitate our Blessed Mother's response of faith and trust in God, the Word takes on flesh once more—

within us and within our world—in ways every bit as real as He did more than two thousand years ago in the tiny village of Nazareth.

Sometimes we forget that Our Lord's genealogy did not cease with His conception and birth. Through the grace of Baptism, which makes His redemptive incarnation and paschal mystery available to us, we have the high privilege of standing in that noble line. We show ourselves worthy of that honor by being identified with Jesus' Mother—a woman who shared the human condition but who was so focused on her God that He was able to use her to undo the negative spiral of human history to that point. God wants to use us in exactly the same way today.

May Mary, Mother of Christ and Mother of Church, intercede with her Son, our Brother, to enable us to respond with faith, with hope, and with love—to reverse our contemporary negative spiral.

⌘

He who charges us with making Mary a divinity, is thereby denying the divinity of Jesus. Such a man does not know what divinity is.... To her belongs, as being a creature, a natural claim on our sympathy and familiarity, in that she is nothing else than our fellow. She is our pride, in the poet's words, "Our tainted nature's solitary boast."[3]

THE PRESENTATION OF THE BLESSED VIRGIN MARY

The Presentation of the Blessed Virgin Mary is celebrated liturgically in the Church Universal on November 21, and commemorates her being brought to live in the sacred precincts of the Temple as a young girl, as the lot had fallen to her to make its purple and scarlet veil. The story is not recounted in Sacred Scripture nor is there any evidence that having girls live at the Temple was practiced; the feast comes from apocryphal sources and has its origins in Eastern Christianity from around the fourth century. Its antiquity suggests at least a very early "intuition" that Our Lady's life, from early childhood forward, was marked out in unique ways as a kind of preparation for the uniqueness it would assume with her divine motherhood.

Whether or not the child Mary was physically presented in the Temple, we have good reason to trust that her holy parents spiritually presented her to the Lord, most particularly in offering her the family and religious environment that enabled her to become, as St. Luke later described, the woman who pondered the Word of God and kept it (Luke 2:19; 8:21). We could say that her dwelling in the spiritual Temple of the Lord during her childhood and adolescence provided the appropriate prelude to her becoming the very Temple itself in which the Son of God Incarnate would make His dwelling for nine months.

The Byzantine liturgy for this feast of the Presentation sings out:

> Today the temple of God's dwelling, the Mother of God, is brought into the Lord's Temple and Zechariah welcomes her. Today the most holy place rejoices, and the angel host keeps mystic festival. We too celebrate with them today, and with Gabriel we cry out: Greetings, favored one! The Lord is with you, who has abundant mercy.

❧

Such was the garden in which the Mystical Rose, the Immaculate Mary, was sheltered and nursed to be the Mother of the All-Holy God, from her birth to her espousals to St. Joseph, a term of thirteen years. For three years of it she was in the arms of her holy mother, St. Anne, and then for ten years she lived in the Temple of God. In those blessed gardens, as they may be called, she lived by herself, continually visited by the dew of God's grace, and growing up a more and more heavenly flower, till at the end of that period she was meet for the inhabitation in her of the Most Holy.[4]

MARY AS A CHILD

Although we have no certain information on the childhood of the Blessed Virgin, we can make some speculations with a degree of assuredness.

First, a commonsense adage: "The apple doesn't fall far from the tree," meaning that children tend to reflect the attitudes and behavior patterns of their parents. Mary's parents did not emerge as accidents of time and space; rather, we must believe that the Heavenly Father chose with great care the man and the woman who would give birth to the girl who would, in turn, give birth to His own Divine Son—which is to say they would have been pious and righteous. Living in the holy "fear of the Lord" and observant of His commands, they would have communicated all this to their little girl. And so Mary would have shone forth with a beauty of soul, befitting her future vocation, and evident in every aspect of her being. Therefore her beauty of soul was likely accompanied by physical beauty.

The physical beauty of Mary, of course, would have been perfectly transmitted to Jesus since all His genetic material came from her. Thus, He was "the perfect Man" in every way—truly the New Adam, in Whom and through Whom the restoration of Eden would occur. Not without reason, then, do the evangelists Matthew and Luke offer us a genealogy for Christ, demonstrating that even

from a purely human perspective He came from an impressive
family tree.

∽◦◦

*But in regarding Mary, we look to one whose actions we know not of
and cannot, if we would, too closely imitate, whose name only recalls to
us bright and pleasant thoughts, the emblem of early devotedness to
God, guiltless piety, angelic purity, meekness, modesty and patience,
shining only in the light of her Son and in the ineffable radiance of that
Spirit of power Who came upon her and overshadowed her, and hence
receiving the prize of that high salutation of Gabriel: "Hail, thou that
art highly favoured (filled with divine gifts), the Lord is with thee,
blessed art thou among women."*[5]

*As regards the Blessed Mary, a further thought suggests itself. She has no
chance place in the Divine Dispensation; the Word of God did not merely
come to her and go from her; He did not pass through her, as He visits us
in Holy Communion. It was no heavenly body which the Eternal Son
assumed, fashioned by the angels, and brought down to this lower world:
no; He imbibed, He absorbed into His Divine Person, her blood and the
substance of her flesh; by becoming man of her, He received her linea-
ments and features, as the appropriate character in which He was to man-
ifest Himself to mankind. The child is like the parent, and we may well
suppose that by His likeness to her was manifested her relationship to
Him. Her sanctity comes, not only of her being His mother, but also of
His being her son. "If the first fruit be holy," says St. Paul, "the mass also
is holy; if the mass be holy, so are the branches." And hence the titles
which we are accustomed to give her. He is the Wisdom of God, she therefore is the Seat of Wisdom; His Presence is Heaven, she therefore is the
Gate of Heaven; He is infinite Mercy, she then is the Mother of Mercy.
She is the Mother of "fair love and fear, and knowledge and holy hope";
is it wonderful then that she has left behind her in the Church below "an
odour like cinnamon and balm, and sweetness like to choice myrrh"?*[6]

THE CEREMONY OF THE RODS

Like Mary's Presentation in the Temple, so too is this story found in the *Protoevangelium of St. James*, which is to say that it may well be a mix of pious imaginings and some kernel of historical accuracy.

This apocryphal gospel tells us that little Mary lived in the Temple until the age of twelve, at which point the priests became concerned that as she moved toward womanhood, with its attendant physical signs (especially menstruation), she would be a source of defilement to the Temple and its sacrifices. It is important to recall that all blood was abhorrent to the Jews of old, not just that of a woman. At any rate, we are told that Zechariah went into the Holy of Holies to consult the Lord God on the fate of the young virgin, with the result that "an angel of the Lord stood by him, saying unto him: 'Zachariah, Zachariah, go out and assemble the widowers of the people, and let them bring each his rod; and to whomsoever the Lord shall show a sign, his wife shall she be'" (*Prot. Jas.*, n. 8).

Joseph joined all the other men. They presented their rods to the High Priest, who prayed over the rods in the Temple and then returned them to the men. He received no sign from any of them, until he came to Joseph, from whose rod there issued forth a dove that rested over Joseph's head, causing the priest to declare: "Thou hast been chosen by lot to take into thy keeping the virgin of the Lord." Joseph protested, saying: "I have children, and I am an old man, and she is a young girl. I am afraid lest I become a laughingstock to the sons of Israel" (*Prot. Jas.*, n. 9). The priest warned Joseph about other men who had questioned or opposed God's will in salvation history, which brought him to obedience as he accepted the young virgin into his life and home.

❦

17

Hence it was, if Mary had been as other women, she would have longed for marriage, as opening on her the prospect of bearing the great King. But she was too humble and too pure for such thoughts. She had been inspired to choose that better way of serving God which had not been made known to the Jews—the state of virginity. She preferred to be His Spouse to being His Mother. Accordingly, when the Angel Gabriel announced to her her high destiny, she shrank from it till she was assured that it would not oblige her to revoke her purpose of a virgin life devoted to her God.[7]

THE ANNUNCIATION

The Solemnity of the Annunciation (March 25) celebrates the high-water point in the history of salvation and is reflected on in the First Joyful Mystery of the Rosary. As we think back on how the greatest event in human history occurred, we stand in awe: the omnipotent God wanted and awaited human cooperation. God the Father made His plan for our salvation contingent on a human being's saying "yes." And so, Our Lady stands as a constant reminder of the great things that can happen when the human person cooperates with the divine initiative. But what she did and what God did through her was not a kind of "one-day sale"; the Lord intends that this happen in the life of every believer. As St. Augustine put it so powerfully: "God made you without your consent but He does not justify you without your consent."[8] Our participation is crucial for our salvation. We don't buy into the Reformation notion of "imputed righteousness," which holds that God "declares us right," even though we really aren't. No, God makes us right because we want to be right—because we respond to His grace to become right and, therefore, do in fact become right in His sight. The Mother of the Word Incarnate is our model in this endeavor, but she is also our faithful intercessor before the throne of her Divine Son.

In the Annunciation, we also learn how to cooperate with the Lord from within the Church, which is—as Sacred Scripture teaches—both Christ's Bride (Eph 5:32) and our Mother (Gal 4:26). The Holy Church, like Holy Mary, always says "yes" to her Bridegroom, and good children always follow their Mother's good example.

Last but not least, the mystery of the Annunciation etches into our consciousness an indefatigable conviction regarding the sanctity of human life—from conception to natural death. God began the work of our redemption at the very moment that the Holy Spirit overshadowed the Virgin Mary and the Eternal Word began His life on Earth in her womb, "pitching His tent among us," as a literal translation of St. John's poetic Greek would have it (John 1:14). This fact of life and faith makes Christians a people of life, ready to promote the cause of life at every turn and equally ready to do battle with a culture of death. Those who want to kill babies in their mothers' wombs and those who want to kill the sick and the elderly cannot know the meaning of the Incarnation and cannot hope to benefit from its saving effects.

The Annunciation, then, stands at the center of the drama of salvation: without the Annunciation, no cross and resurrection; without the Annunciation, no Church or sacraments; without the Annunciation, no eternal life on high with God. In a marvelous even if fanciful re-creation of the visit of the Archangel Gabriel to Our Lady, St. Bernard of Clairvaux caught the essence of what was really at stake on that first Annunciation Day: The whole of creation was waiting to be redeemed, hanging on the response of the Virgin of Nazareth. He says:

> You have heard, O Virgin, that you will conceive and bear a son; you have heard that it will not be by man but by the Holy Spirit. The Angel awaits an answer; it is

time for him to return to God Who sent him....Answer quickly, O Virgin. Reply in haste to the Angel, or rather through the Angel to the Lord. Answer with a word, receive the Word of God. Speak your own word, conceive the divine Word. Breathe a passing word, embrace the eternal Word.[9]

❧

This great title may be fitly connected with the Maternity of Mary, that is, with the coming upon her of the Holy Ghost at Nazareth after the Angel Gabriel's annunciation to her, and with the consequent birth of Our Lord at Bethlehem. She, as the Mother of Our Lord, comes nearer to Him than any angel; nearer even than the Seraphim who surround Him, and cry continually, "Holy, Holy, Holy."

...St. Gabriel hailed her as "Full of grace," and as "Blessed among women," and announced to her that the Holy Ghost would come down upon her, and that she would bear a Son Who would be the Son of the Highest.[10]

HAIL, MARY

Catholics seek Mary's intercession just as they seek the intercession of all good Christians, living and dead—for all are alive in Christ (1 Cor 15:22). This Christian concern for one another manifested through intercessory prayer is as old as the Church. So if we, who still sin, can pray effectively for one another, why not the saints in glory?

The favorite prayer of Christians to the Mother of Christ is the Ave Maria, so often the inspiration for great musical compositions. The words are simple:

> Hail, Mary, full of grace, the Lord is with thee; blessed
> art thou among women, and blessed is the fruit of thy
> womb, Jesus. Holy Mary, Mother of God, pray for us
> sinners, now and at the hour of our death. Amen.

What could any "Bible-believing" Christian find objectionable in a prayer whose roots are so biblical? The first half is a direct quote from Luke (1:28, 42), while the second half contains the Church's affirmations of the divinity of Christ, the fallen state of man, human mortality, and the power of intercessory prayer.

The Hail Mary is sometimes referred to as the "angelic salutation" because it was how the Archangel Gabriel (whose name means "God is strong") greeted Mary to announce God's plan and purpose, into which he invited her participation and cooperation. The Greek word St. Luke uses, which is traditionally translated into English as "full of grace," is a powerful one, signifying both possessing and being thoroughly possessed by God's grace and favor. Hearing such a description applied to herself would have given the young virgin the necessary confidence to respond with the totality of her being: "Let it be to me according to your word" (Luke 2:38).

The second greeting comes from Mary's kinswoman Elizabeth, who uttered what could be considered the first "beatitude," or blessing, of the New Testament. Under the direct influence of the Holy Spirit, St. Luke tells us, she declares "blessed" both Mary and the Child she is carrying (Luke 2:42). Elizabeth then concluded with yet another beatitude as she praised her cousin's faith: "And blessed is she who believed that there would be a fulfillment of what was spoken to her from the Lord" (Luke 1:45).

As can be readily seen, the Holy Spirit wants us to hold Our Lady in high esteem and to regard all her grace and blessedness as flowing from her faith and from her Divine Son.

✎

We see then the force of Our Lady's title when we call her "Holy Mary." When God would prepare a human mother for His Son, this was why He began by giving her an immaculate conception. He began, not by giving her the gift of love, or truthfulness, or gentleness, or devotion, though according to the occasion she had them all. But He began His great work before she was born; before she could think, speak, or act, by making her holy, and thereby, while on earth, a citizen of Heaven. "Tota pulchra es, Maria!" Nothing of the deformity of sin was ever hers. Thus she differs from all saints. There have been great missionaries, confessors, bishops, doctors, pastors. They have done great works, and have taken with them numberless converts or penitents to Heaven. They have suffered much, and have a superabundance of merits to show. But Mary in this way resembles her Divine Son, viz., that, as He, being God, is separate by holiness from all creatures, so she is separate from all saints and angels, as being "full of grace."[11]

THE VISITATION

Mary's visit to her kinswoman Elizabeth is recounted in the Gospel according to St. Luke (1:39–45), is celebrated liturgically in the Latin Church on May 3, and is meditated on as the Second Joyful Mystery of the Rosary. There is much to ponder in this event, but let two thoughts suffice for the moment.

First, notice what happened when Our Lady conceived the Lord and Messiah in her virginal womb: the pregnant Mary, with evangelical immediacy, launched out on an arduous and perhaps even dangerous journey to tend to her elderly cousin, who had also experienced God's mercy through a miraculous (even if not virginal) conception. Mary exhibited selfless charity and an intense commitment to share the Gospel message with every person. Evangelization and charity have been the hallmarks of every true disciple of the Lord ever since, as they emulate the life and witness of the first and best Christian ever to live.

Second, who could not be touched by the sacred conversation that took place between the two infants in the wombs of their respective mothers? The man who would be known as John the Baptist sensed the presence of the Redeemer and, St. Elizabeth told the Blessed Virgin, "leaped for joy." Thus, we see—already from the womb—that Precursor and Messiah are in communication, eventually leading the former to proclaim of the latter: "Behold the Lamb of God, who takes away the sin of the world!" (John 1:29). In this culture of death that gnaws away at the so-called developed countries of the world, the moving "dialogue" between the two unborn infants is truly a reminder of the assertion of the Prophet Jeremiah, "Before I formed you in the womb I knew you, / before you were born I dedicated you: / a prophet to the nations I appointed you" (1:5).

✧

But why [is Mary] called a house or palace? And whose palace? She is the house and the palace of the Great King, of God Himself. Our Lord, the Co-equal Son of God, once dwelt in her. He was her Guest; nay, more than a guest, for a guest comes into a house as well as leaves it. But Our Lord was actually born in this holy house. He took His flesh and His blood from this house, from the flesh, from the veins of Mary. Rightly then was she made to be of pure gold, because she was to give of that gold to form the Body of the Son of God. She was golden in her conception, golden in her birth. She went through the fire of her suffering like gold in the furnace, and when she ascended on high, she was, in the words of our hymn,

Above all the Angels in glory untold,
Standing next to the King in a vesture of gold.[12]

THE *MAGNIFICAT*

The Gospel according to St. Luke is notable in that it gives us three canticles to which the Church has recourse in her daily prayer known as the Liturgy of the Hours: the *Benedictus* of Zechariah (1:68–79), which is chanted at Lauds, or morning prayer; the *Magnificat* of Our Lady (1:46–55), which is sung at Vespers, or evening prayer; and the *Nunc Dimittis* of Simeon (2:29–32), which at Compline, or night prayer, closes the Church's day of praise for the Triune God. Luke makes a point of indicating that the two men uttered their hymns after an inspiration of the Holy Spirit. For Our Lady, he merely writes, "And Mary said…" The implication would seem to be that no direct intervention of the Holy Spirit was necessary because Mary was, from the very first moment of her existence, possessed of the Holy Spirit. As such, she is *the* prophetess, who speaks God's Word and who lives and presents a Spirit-filled life.

And so, Mary's canticle of praise reveals a woman steeped in the Sacred Scriptures as she took the canticle of Hannah (1 Sam 2:1–10) and applied those lines to herself, in whom she saw them admirably fulfilled. She likewise exhibited a strong sense of the sovereignty of God, to Whom she referred all her greatness.

As *the* woman of the Holy Spirit par excellence, Mary prophesied that "all generations to come shall call me blessed." Catholics deem it both an obligation and a privilege to fulfill that prophecy— as should any Bible-believing Christian. One would not be impertinent to ask how a Christian who takes the Scriptures seriously could be anything but a devotee of the Blessed Virgin, exalted by her kinswoman Elizabeth in the lead-up to Mary's canticle and thus the first of millions of believers to call her "blessed."

The Gospel of Luke could be considered the first Mariological tract in Christian theology, as well as the first tract on the Person and mission of the Holy Spirit, Who dots the pages of the third Gospel. That same Spirit, we learn, is the source of joy in the life of the disciple. No surprise, then, to hear Mary exclaim, "My spirit finds *joy* in God my Savior."

The Holy Spirit…Mary…joy. If Our Lady is truly the ideal disciple, the one who hears the Word of God, reflects on it, and acts upon it through the Holy Spirit's presence within her, then she should likewise be the very paradigm of Christian joy. Joy is to be distinguished from any type of superficial hilarity. Rather, it is the quality that enables us to live our lives here below with calmness and serenity. Hence, six times during St. John's account of the Last Supper (chapters 15–17), we hear Our Lord exhort His disciples to live in joy—a joy, He asserts, that no one can take from us (John 16:22). St. Paul would even command his flock to "rejoice in the Lord always" (Phil 4:4)—a line that became the Introit, or Entrance Antiphon, for Gaudete Sunday (the Third Sunday in Advent), while its companion verse (Isa 66:10) does similar duty for Laetare Sunday (the Fourth Sunday in Lent). It suggests to us that even in a penitential spirit, the true disciple will have cause to rejoice. Why? Because we view things *sub specie aeternitatis* ("from the perspective of eternity"), that is, from the vantage point of all things in Christ, Who has won the victory for us and in us.

Undoubtedly, this was the joy with which the Blessed Virgin was imbued throughout all the vicissitudes of her own earthly pilgrimage, as well as the earthly life and ministry of her dear Son, which themselves became her own joys and sorrows. With that kind of mind-set, we can see why the Church wisely invokes her in the Litany of Loreto as the "cause of our joy."

25

❦

Who can repeat her very name without finding in it a music which goes to the heart, and brings before him thoughts of God and Jesus Christ, and Heaven above, and fills him with the desire of those graces by which Heaven is gained?

Hail then, great Mother of God, Queen of Saints, Royal Lady clothed with the sun and crowned with the stars of Heaven, whom all generations have called and shall call blessed. We will take our part in praising thee in our own time and place with all the redeemed of Our Lord, and will exalt thee in the full assembly of the saints and glorify thee in the Heavenly Jerusalem.[13]

EN ROUTE TO BETHLEHEM

When St. Paul informs us that God's Son came among us "in the fullness of time" (Eph 1:10), he is reminding us that the plan of our salvation was no haphazard situation. Rather, it was guided by the loving hand of Providence to when the three great cultures of Greece, Rome, and Israel had coalesced to form the *chairos* (the "precise right moment") for the God-Man to make His appearance on the human stage. And so, God used even the political decrees of Caesar Augustus to get Mary and Joseph to Bethlehem, so that the birth of the Child could take place in fulfillment of the prophecy of Micah: "But you, O Bethlehem Ephrathah, / who are little to be among the clans of Judah, / from you shall come forth for me / one who is to be ruler in Israel" (Mic 5:2).

Besides the fulfillment of prophecy, why was it important for the Messiah and Lord to be born in that tiny, backwater town? Names were critically important in the biblical world, and the name of this town was no exception. *Bethlehem* means "House of

Bread." How significant it is for the One Who would identify Himself as the Bread of Life (John 6:35) to be born there. From His very birthplace, we are invited to join a Eucharistic procession, with Mary as the veritable "woman of the Eucharist," as Pope John Paul II was so fond of speaking of her. That procession would find its Eucharistic culmination on Calvary, with the virgins Mary and John joined in a holy union by the virginal Great High Priest from the altar of His Cross.

I say then, when once we have mastered the idea, that Mary bore, suckled, and handled the Eternal in the form of a child, what limit is conceivable to the rush and flood of thoughts which such a doctrine involves? What awe and surprise must attend upon the knowledge, that a creature has been brought so close to the Divine Essence?...It was the creation of a new idea and of a new sympathy, of a new faith and worship, when the holy Apostles announced that God had become incarnate; then a supreme love and devotion to Him became possible, which seemed hopeless before that revelation.[14]

THE NATIVITY OF OUR LORD

Most traditional artistic depictions of nativity scenes are suffused with calmness and serenity, but I suspect the reality was quite otherwise. In fact, tension, confusion, anxiety, and a great deal of inconvenience might be far closer to the reality.

Thomas Merton in his poem "The Messenger" characterizes Our Lady's reaction to the message of the Archangel Gabriel as both loving and dreading it: loving it because her great faith enabled her to see that her cooperation would lead to the salvation of the world; dreading it because she knew how difficult it would all be for her and for her Son. Those same sentiments would have carried over into all the other experiences related to the Child's impending birth, infancy, and childhood. Of course, these feelings of apprehension were not unique to the Blessed Virgin; all mothers know them to a greater or lesser degree, but they would have been particularly acute for her because of what was at stake—nothing less than the salvation of the world to be wrought by her Son. Moreover, that salvation would be opposed by Satan, who would do everything possible to thwart its achievement.

When meditating on these eventualities, can we not suppose that Our Lady had recourse to Genesis 3:15? Theologians term this passage the Protoevangelium, or first proclamation of the Gospel, because the sacred author spoke of a future redemption:

> "I will put enmity between you and the woman,
>   and between your seed and her seed;
> he shall bruise your head,
>   and you shall bruise his heel."

And so, the child of the woman prophesied in the Protoevangelium would do decisive battle with the Evil One, but Satan would not be victorious ultimately: if all you can do is strike at someone's heel while he can crush your skull, the outcome is clear. Some translations have the pronoun *she* (Mary), instead of *he* (Jesus), for the subject of the verb *shall bruise*. Interestingly, the translation offered by the Jewish Publication Society of America has *they*. If that translation is the most accurate, it would suggest a wonderful collaboration between Jesus as the Second Adam and Mary as the Second Eve, who cooperates with her Son in the work of our redemption. This is precisely why Irenaeus and other Fathers of the Church gave the Blessed Virgin the title of Second Eve: the harm caused by the first Eve was to be undone by a better and second Eve, the one whom Cardinal Newman called "the daughter of Eve unfallen"[15]—the sinless Mother of the sinless Lamb of God.

The redemption of the world was not limited to one moment: indeed, the entire Christ-event was salvific; otherwise, why would the Father have sent His Son to tarry among us for thirty or more years? His virginal conception, birth, and saving death form a unity, which would be a source of concern and consternation to Satan. The *Catechism of the Catholic Church* cites an early Father of the Church in this regard: "St. Ignatius of Antioch already bears witness to this connection: 'Mary's virginity and giving birth and even the Lord's death escaped the notice of the prince of this world: these three mysteries worthy of proclamation were accomplished in God's silence'" (*CCC* 498). And what do these three mysteries have in common? The presence of Our Lady, fulfilling the prophetic word of Genesis 3:15.

That presence of Our Lady is brought into sharp focus so often in medieval and Renaissance art as Mother and Child gaze upon each other lovingly with delightful smiles. No wonder that Christians of the Middle Ages (following the lead of Dante and of Eusebius of Caesarea) took as nearly prophetic the Fourth Eclogue of the Roman master poet Virgil, in which we are told of a child (the poet had in mind Caesar Augustus) who would usher in a new age of peace. Christians heard in such lines a remarkable echo of Isaiah's prophecy that "a little child shall lead them" (11:6). Most of all, they were captivated by this particular line from the Eclogue: "Begin, O little boy, to recognize your mother by her smile."

❧

In her [Mary] the destinies of the world were to be reversed, and the serpent's head bruised. On her was bestowed the greatest honour ever put upon any individual of our fallen race.... In her the curse pronounced on Eve was changed to a blessing.[16]

In that awful transaction [the fall of man] there were three parties concerned, the serpent, the woman, and the man; and at the time of their sentence, an event was announced for a distant future, in which the three same parties were to meet again, the serpent, the woman, and the man; but it was to be a second Adam and a second Eve, and the new Eve was to be the mother of the new Adam. "I will put enmity between thee and the woman, and between thy seed and her seed." The Seed of the woman is the Word Incarnate, and the Woman, whose seed or Son He is, is His Mother Mary.[17]

THE ADORATION OF THE SHEPHERDS

What Child is this who, laid to rest
On Mary's lap is sleeping?
Whom Angels greet with anthems sweet,
While shepherds watch are keeping?
This, this is Christ the King,
Whom shepherds guard and Angels sing;
Haste, haste, to bring Him laud,
The Babe, the Son of Mary.

Why lies He in such mean estate,
Where ox and ass are feeding?
Good Christians, fear, for sinners here
The silent Word is pleading.
Nails, spear shall pierce Him through,
The Cross be borne for me, for you.
Hail, hail the Word made flesh,
The Babe, the Son of Mary.

This lilting carol brings into focus St. Luke's depiction of that first Christmas night with Mary, her Son, and the shepherds (Luke 2:8–20). The spot identified by immemorial tradition as Jesus' birthplace is now marked by the Basilica of the Nativity in Bethlehem. To enter, one must bend down to get in. The historical reason for why the door was made low is that then invading Muslim horsemen could not enter! With the passage of time and Christian reflection, that means of access was dubbed the "Door of Humility," reminding all that to gain access spiritually to the mystery of the Incarnation, one has to be humble enough to let faith take over when reason reaches its limits. As Archbishop Fulton Sheen put it in his autobiography, *Treasure in Clay*: "Humility is always the condition for discovering divinity; divinity seems always to be where one least expects it."[18] The shepherds were the first visitors to the cave of Bethlehem, and they epitomized the humility that Archbishop Sheen praised in those "who know nothing and those who know they do not know everything."[19]

In his magisterial *Life of Christ*, Archbishop Sheen also noted that "every other person who ever came into this world came into it to live. He came into it to die."[20] That theme is hit upon in the carol as well. To look at a God-Man hanging in agony on a cross takes a certain suspension of belief and a humility that enables one to be educated by the wisdom of God, rather than men. "For the word of the cross is folly to those who are perishing, but to us who are being saved, it is the power of God. For it is written, 'I will destroy the wisdom of the wise, and the cleverness of the clever I will thwart'" (1 Cor 1:18–19).

There is another spot in the Holy Land that requires one to bend very low to enter, and that is the Holy Sepulcher. Yes, to attempt to fathom the mystery of the Resurrection demands the same humility that allows one to revel in the mystery of the Incarnation, in which are enfolded an unassuming birth and an ignominious death.

What Mary Means to Christians

Humble Virgin of Nazareth, pray for us, that we may be made worthy of the promises of Christ, your Incarnate and Risen Son.

❦

"The shepherds said one to another, Let us now go even unto Bethlehem, and see this thing which is come to pass, which the Lord hath made known to us." Let us too go with them, to contemplate that second and greater miracle to which the Angel directed them, the Nativity of Christ. St. Luke says of the Blessed Virgin, "She brought forth her first-born Son, and wrapped Him in swaddling clothes, and laid Him in a manger." What a wonderful sign is this to all the world, and therefore the Angel repeated it to the shepherds: "Ye shall find the babe wrapped in swaddling clothes, lying in a manger." The God of heaven and earth, the Divine Word, Who had been in glory with the Eternal Father from the beginning, He was at this time born into this world of sin as a little infant. He, as at this time, lay in His mother's arms, to all appearance helpless and powerless, and was wrapped by Mary in an infant's bands, and laid to sleep in a manger. The Son of God Most High, who created the worlds, became flesh, though remaining what He was before. He became flesh as truly as if He had ceased to be what He was, and had actually been changed into flesh. He submitted to be the offspring of Mary, to be taken up in the hands of a mortal, to have a mother's eye fixed upon Him, and to be cherished at a mother's bosom. A daughter of man became the Mother of God—to her, indeed, an unspeakable gift of grace; but in Him what condescension! What an emptying of His glory to become man! and not only a helpless infant, though that were humiliation enough, but to inherit all the infirmities and imperfections of our nature which were possible to a sinless soul. What were His thoughts, if we may venture to use such language or admit such a reflection concerning the Infinite, when human feelings, human sorrows, human wants, first became His? What a mystery is there from first to last in the Son of God becoming man! Yet in proportion to the mystery is the grace and mercy of it; and as is the grace, so is the greatness of the fruit of it.[21]

THE ADORATION OF THE MAGI

The visit of the Magi is recorded only by St. Matthew, who laconically remarks that the intriguing visitors found the "child with Mary his mother" (2:11). By this point in the infancy narratives, we discover that the Holy Family is now living in a house. The liturgical feast of the visit of the Magi is celebrated traditionally on January 6, but is transferred to the nearest Sunday if it is not a holy day of obligation in a region. The feast is called the Solemnity of the Epiphany (Greek for "revelation"). In the pre–Vatican II calendar, there was a season of Epiphanytide, wherein three epiphanies ("manifestations") were commemorated. These have been enshrined in the lovely hymn "Songs of Thankfulness and Praise": the manifestation of Jesus to the Magi, representing the Gentile world; the manifestation of Jesus as the Beloved Son of the Father at His Baptism in the Jordan; and the manifestation of His glory in the performance of His first sign at the wedding feast of Cana. Two of the three epiphanies are still observed in the revised calendar, while the third comes up only during Cycle C of the lectionary.

The delightful hymns for the feast of the Epiphany are not only moving reflections on this mystery but also highly instructive. In this regard, "We Three Kings" is most helpful, for the gifts these "wise men" bring (to what we may think of as the first Christian baby shower) are revelatory in a special way for the Virgin Mother.

Sometimes people operate from the presumption that Our Lady had the whole package presented to her by the Angel Gabriel at the Annunciation, but that does not do justice to what the Council Fathers of Vatican II referred to as Mary's "pilgrimage of faith" (*Lumen Gentium*, n. 58); nor does that help us, her sons and daughters, as we wend our way Heavenward. No, each day of her life here below required a renewal of her initial *fiat*, just as each day requires of us a renewal of our baptismal commitment.

So, what did those gifts reveal to Mary—and to us? They gave her a sneak preview of her future joys and sorrows. The Infant was King (gold), Priest (frankincense), and Lamb of Sacrifice (myrrh). Surely, a mother could raise a hearty "Amen" to the first two, but to the third? Here she must have returned in her mind's eye to the Temple scene not many days before, when the old man Simeon prophesied about a sword piercing her heart (Luke 2:35). It seems that joy tinged with sorrow (or even overladen with sorrow) was the pattern for the Blessed Mother: Simeon declares the Child responsible for the rise of many in Israel, but also for the fall of many; the adolescent Jesus is found among the doctors of the Law in the Temple, but He then reminds His Mother that His real place is not with her; she brims with pride as He enthralls the multitudes with His preaching, but then hears rumblings of dissatisfaction.

In that roller-coaster existence of being the Blessed Mother of the "Savior, who is Christ the Lord" (Luke 2:11), her faith was regularly put to the test. That is why, many years hence, when an enthusiastic woman shouted out to Jesus a beatitude for his Mother—"Blessed is the womb that bore you, and the breasts that you sucked"—he issued a corrective: "Blessed rather are those who hear the word of God and keep it!" (Luke 11:27–28). This was not an ungrateful Son's attempt to diminish His Mother's identity and role; on the contrary, it was an attempt to elevate her to a higher position. St. Luke had already told us that Mary was a firm believer (1:45) and likewise one who meditated on the mysteries with which she was involved (2:51). Our Lord did not want people to engage in some cheap form of ancestor worship of Mary simply because she was His Mother; no, He wanted her to be numbered among and, indeed, numbered the first of His truest disciples. Thus does St. Augustine wisely comment that the Blessed Virgin was "more blessed in believing than in conceiving."[22]

With good reason, then, does traditional iconography for the Epiphany depict the Mother "presenting" the Child to the Magi— a task she happily fulfills for any and all heirs to those Wise Men who were seeking truth: Truth Incarnate.

❧

The Virgin and Child is not a mere modern idea; on the contrary, it is represented again and again, as every visitor to Rome is aware, in the paintings of the Catacombs. Mary is there drawn with the Divine Infant in her lap, she with hands extended in prayer, He with His hand in the attitude of blessing. No representation can more forcibly convey the doctrine of the high dignity of the Mother, and, I will add, of her influence with her Son. Why should the memory of His time of subjection be so dear to Christians, and so carefully preserved? The only question to be determined, is the precise date of these remarkable monuments of the first age of Christianity. That they belong to the centuries of what Anglicans call the "undivided Church" is certain; but lately investigations have been pursued, which place some of them at an earlier date than any one anticipated as possible. I am not in a position to quote largely from the works of the Cavaliere de Rossi, who has thrown so much light upon the subject; but I have his "Imagini Scelte," published in 1863, and they are sufficient for my purpose. In this work he has given us from the Catacombs various representations of the Virgin and Child; the latest of these belong to the early part of the fourth century, but the earliest he believes to be referable to the very age of the Apostles. He comes to this conclusion from the style and the skill of its composition, and from the history, locality, and existing inscriptions of the subterranean in which it is found. However, he does not go so far as to insist upon so early a date; yet the utmost concession he makes is to refer the painting to the era of the first Antonines, that is, to a date within half a century of the death of St. John. I consider then, that, as you would use in controversy with Protestants, and fairly, the traditional doctrine of the Church in early times, as an explanation of a particular passage of

*Scripture, or at least as a suggestion, or as a defence, of the sense which
you may wish to put upon it, quite apart from the question whether your
interpretation itself is directly traditional, so it is lawful for me, though
I have not the positive words of the Fathers on my side, to shelter my own
interpretation of the Apostle's vision in the Apocalypse under the fact of
the extant pictures of Mother and Child in the Roman Catacombs.*[23]

THE FLIGHT INTO EGYPT

Insensitivity and genuine cruelty in political figures are not a novelty
of modernity. The flight of the Holy Family into Egypt (Matt
2:13–23) was precipitated precisely by the paranoia of Herod, who
valued the maintenance of his own power more than the life of a
newborn baby who posed a potential threat to that power. As a result,
he was willing to sacrifice the life of not just one boy-child but of any
and all who could have stood in the way of his corrupt reign. A sad
but incontrovertible fact of life is that Herod has many descendants
in contemporary politics as millions of new "Holy Innocents" are
offered up on the altars of political expediency through abortion.

At any rate, as the proverb teaches us, God can "write straight
with crooked lines." And so, He uses the perversity of Herod to
have the Holy Family live in Egypt, probably in Alexandria, that
great center of Jewish life in the Diaspora, so that the Boy Jesus
would come to learn of Greek language and culture, thus preparing
Him to be what old Simeon prophesied: "A light for revelation to
the Gentiles and for glory to thy people Israel" (Luke 2:32).

At the same time, this experience of exile and persecution
makes Mary and Joseph ideal patrons of all refugees, especially
those driven from their homelands due to religious persecution.
And that is why the Church's maternal heart has always had a special affection for such people and why she expects all her children to

reach out to refugees and migrants, particularly to those who "belong to the household of faith" (Gal 6:10). The anxiety of alienation from one's native and familiar surroundings was truly one of the seven sorrows of Our Lady, again foretold by Simeon as he warned her that "a sword will pierce through your own soul also" (Luke 2:35).

∽

And she especially can console us because she suffered more than mothers in general. Women, at least delicate women, are commonly shielded from rude experience of the highways of the world; but she, after Our Lord's Ascension, was sent out into foreign lands almost as the Apostles were, a sheep among wolves. In spite of all St. John's care of her, which was as great as was St. Joseph's in her younger days, she, more than all the saints of God, was a stranger and a pilgrim upon earth, in proportion to her greater love of Him Who had been on earth, and had gone away. As, when Our Lord was an Infant, she had to flee across the desert to the heathen Egypt, so, when He had ascended on high, she had to go on shipboard to the heathen Ephesus, where she lived and died.

O ye who are in the midst of rude neighbours or scoffing companions, or of wicked acquaintances, or of spiteful enemies, and are helpless, invoke the aid of Mary by the memory of her own sufferings among the heathen Greeks and the heathen Egyptians.[24]

THE FINDING IN THE TEMPLE

Any time I proclaim the Gospel of the loss of the Child Jesus, I notice mothers in the congregation develop a worried look on their faces, which changes to a smile as the story concludes with His finding! Yes, Our Lady was a mother who experienced all the anxieties and all the joys of every other mother. There's a degree of pique in her voice as she upbraids the wayward Boy: "Son, why have you treated us so? Behold, your father and I have been looking for you anxiously" (Luke 2:48). The Reformer John Calvin has an appealing defense of the Blessed Mother's comment: "The weariness of three days was in that complaint," he explained.

Noting Calvin's defense gives us a good opportunity to mention that the original Protestant Reformers did not have knee-jerk, allergic reactions to the Blessed Virgin, as have some of their progeny in recent centuries. Indeed, Martin Luther, John Calvin, and Ulrich Zwingli all accepted the doctrines of Mary's perpetual virginity, immaculate conception, and bodily assumption—even though the last two were not even formally defined dogmas of faith yet!

Reflecting on this passage, I always wonder if Mary came to regard this episode of her twelve-year-old Son teaching the teachers as a foreshadowing; undoubtedly that scene returned in her mind's eye on several occasions as she watched Him teaching the crowds during His public ministry. She was the "Seat of Wisdom": her lap had provided a resting place for Wisdom Incarnate to rest.

Considering how the twelve-year-old Son gently reminds His Mother that He had to be about His Father's affairs, St. Bede the Venerable has this to say in his *Exposition of the Gospel of Luke*:

> Consider the most prudent woman Mary, Mother of true Wisdom, as the pupil of her Son. For she learned from Him, not as from a child or man but as from God. Yes, she dwells in meditation on His words and actions. Nothing of what was said or done by Him fell idly on her mind. As before, when she conceived the Word Itself in her womb, so now does she hold within her His ways and words, cherishing them as it were in her heart. That which she now beholds in the present, she waits to have revealed with greater clarity in the future.

This practice she followed as a rule and law through all her life.[25]

Then, as little more than a codicil to the whole episode, St. Luke observes that the Child Jesus "went down with [Mary and Joseph] and came to Nazareth, and was obedient to them" (2:41). Humility and docility formed a two-way street in the Holy House of Nazareth.

❧

If you would bring out distinctly and beyond mistake and evasion, the simple idea of the Catholic Church that God is man,...could you express this more emphatically and unequivocally than by declaring that He was born a man, or that He had a Mother? *The world allows that God* is *man; the admission costs it little, for God is everywhere, and (as it may say) is everything; but it shrinks from confessing that God is the Son of Mary. It shrinks, for it is at once confronted with a severe fact, which violates and shatters its own unbelieving view of things; the revealed doctrine forthwith takes its true shape, and receives an historical reality; and the Almighty is introduced into His own world at a certain time and in a definite way. Dreams are broken and shadows depart; the divine truth is no longer a poetical expression, or a devotional exaggeration, or a mystical economy, or a mythical representation. "Sacrifice and offering," the shadows of the Law, "Thou wouldest not, but a body hast Thou fitted to me....the confession that Mary is Deipara, or the Mother of God, is that safeguard wherewith we seal up and secure the doctrine of the Apostle from all evasion, and that test whereby we detect all the pretences of those bad spirits of 'Antichrist which have gone out into the world.'" It declares that He is God; it implies that He is man; it suggests to us that He is God still, though He has become man, and that He is true man though He is God. If Mary is the Mother of God, Christ must be literally Emmanuel, God with us. And hence it was, that, when time went on, and the bad spirits and false prophets grew stronger and bolder, and found a way into the Catholic body itself, then the Church, guided by God, could find no more effectual and sure way of expelling them than that of using this word, Deipara, against them; and on the other hand, when they came up again from the realms of darkness and plotted the utter overthrow of Christian faith in the sixteenth century, then they could find no more certain expedient for their hateful purpose than that of reviling and blaspheming the prerogatives of Mary, for they knew full well that, if they could once get the world to dishonour the Mother, the dishonour of the Son would follow close. The Church and Satan agreed together in this, that Son and Mother went together; and the experience of three centuries has confirmed their testimony, for Catholics who have honoured the Mother, still worship the Son, while Protestants, who now have ceased to confess the Son, began then by scoffing at the Mother.*[26]

Mary and the Young Jesus

Rather infrequently do we reflect on the fact that for some (rather long?) period of time, Our Lady and her Divine Son lived under the same roof. The Church celebrates the memorial of the Immaculate Heart of Mary the day after the Solemnity of the Sacred Heart of Jesus—these two feasts are not situated by coincidence but by the careful plan of the Church. The heart of Jesus began beating beneath the heart of His Blessed Mother; her heart, in turn, took form from the creative Word and Power of the Heart of God: two hearts beating as one.

The heart is a symbol with a rich biblical lineage. In Hebrew, both the heart and the bowels represent the very depths of a person—where the cognitive and the affective meet in unity and harmony. Hence, we find passages in the Bible that speak thus: "My heart recoils within me, my compassion grows warm and tender" (Hos 11:8). Far more than just an organ of the body, then, the heart suggests the source of compassion, tenderness, kindness—in short, what we call "mercy." An interesting piece of biblical trivia: A quick survey of a biblical concordance reveals that the word *mercy* is used more than 200 times in Sacred Scripture, while the word *heart* appears over 600 times. No surprise, then, that St. Augustine, playing with the origins of the Latin word for mercy (*misericordia*), tells us that God's grace moves us *"a miseria ad misericordiam"* ("from misery to mercy"). *Misericordia*, it should be noted, comes from two words that combine to mean "having a heart for the miserable."

In *The Merchant of Venice*, Shakespeare rhapsodized about the beauty and glory of mercy when he had Portia exclaim:

> The quality of mercy is not strain'd,
> It droppeth as the gentle rain from heaven
> Upon the place beneath: it is twice blest;
> It blesseth him that gives and him that takes:
> 'Tis mightiest in the mightiest; it becomes
> The throned monarch better than his crown;
> His sceptre shows the force of temporal power,
> The attribute to awe and majesty,
> Wherein doth sit the dread and fear of kings;
> But mercy is above this sceptred sway,
> It is enthroned in the hearts of kings,
> It is an attribute to God Himself,
> And earthly power doth then show likest God's
> When mercy seasons justice. Therefore, Jew,
> Though justice be thy plea, consider this,
> That in the course of justice none of us
> Should see salvation: we do pray for mercy,
> And that same prayer doth teach us all to render
> The deeds of mercy. (IV, i, 180–98)

As beautiful as these words are, someone once observed, "Before Shakespeare wrote it, God was it!"

Indeed, God became Mercy Incarnate within the spotless womb of the Virgin Mary. And she understood it all so well that she broke forth into her canticle of praise, the *Magnificat*: "And his mercy is on those who fear him from generation to generation" (Luke 2:50). Our Lady was not teaching theology from a textbook but giving praise from her own experience of life. God had touched her so profoundly by His mercy that she became what the Church's lovely night prayer, the *Salve Regina*, rightly calls her— *Mater misericordiae* ("Mother of Mercy"). God the Father sought the young maiden's cooperation with His eternal plan of mercy; God the Holy Spirit overshadowed her with His merciful wings; God the Son made her the very seat of Mercy, the Mother of the One Who is *dives in misericordia* ("rich in mercy"; Eph 2:4).

Our world needs to hear the message of mercy perhaps as no other age before. A culture of violence, death, destruction, and despair can be healed only by mercy. We, like St. Faustina Kowalska before us, must count ourselves among the apostles of mercy. But first we must be convinced that mercy has been granted us; otherwise, our words will ring hollow. The result of knowing mercy, which comes from the very core or heart of the Being of God, means being grabbed at the very core or heart of our own being—which gives birth to the emotion (both divine and human) of joy. Once more, Our Lady leads the way as she sings out: "My spirit rejoices in God my Savior" (Luke 2:47). Where mercy spawns joy—melancholy, fear, and death are definitively banished.

May the Mother of Mercy show us the blessed fruit of her womb, Who is none other than the compassionate face of God, Mercy in the flesh.

∽ঔ৩

[St. Peter] Canisius,...while engaged in showing the carefulness with which the Church distinguishes the worship of God from the cultus of the Blessed Virgin, observes, "Lest the Church should depart from Latria

(i.e., the worship of God) she has instituted the public supplications in the Liturgy in perpetuity in such wise as to address them directly to God the Father, and not to the saints, according to that common form of praying, 'Almighty, everlasting God,' &c.; and the said prayers which they also call 'Collects,' she generally ends in this way, 'through Jesus Christ, Thy Son, our Lord.'" He says more to the same purpose; but the two points here laid down are sufficient; viz., that as to the Latin Missal, Ritual, and Breviary, (1) Saints are not directly addressed in these authoritative books; and (2) in them prayers end with the name of Jesus...

Now let us observe how far less observant of dogmatic exactness, how free and fearless in its exaltation of the Blessed Virgin, is the formal Greek [Byzantine] devotion:

1. "We have risen from sleep, and we fall down before Thee, O good God; and we sing to Thee the Angelic Hymn, O powerful God. Holy, holy, holy art Thou, God; have mercy on us through the Theotocos.

"Thou hast raised me from my bed and slumber, O God. Lighten my mind, and open my heart and lips, to sing of Thee, Holy Trinity. Holy, holy, holy art Thou, God; have mercy on us through the Theotocos.

"Soon will come the Judge, and the deeds of all will be laid bare.... Holy, holy, holy art Thou, God; have mercy on us through the Theotocos."...

2. "O God, who lookest on the earth, and makest it tremble, deliver us from the fearful threatenings of earthquake, Christ our God; and send down on us Thy rich mercies, and save us, at the intercessions (presbeiais) *of the Theotocos."...*

24. "Show forth thy speedy protection and aid and mercy on thy servant, and still the waves, thou pure one, of vain thoughts, and raise up my fallen soul, O Mother of God. For I know, O Virgin, I know that thou hast power for whatever thou willest."...

I say then, first: That usage, which, after a split has taken place in a religious communion, is found to obtain equally in each of its separated parts, may fairly be said to have existed before the split occurred.

The concurrence of Orthodox, Nestorian, and Jacobite in the honours they pay to the Blessed Virgin, is an evidence that those honours were in their substance paid to her in their "Undivided Church."[27]

THE HOLY FAMILY

The Second Vatican Council popularized the notion of the family as the "domestic church." The Council intended us to understand thereby that education in faith and an experience of the holy generally and ideally occur within the context of the Christian family. Pope John Paul II never tired of remarking that "civilization passes by way of the family." He was firmly convinced by the witness of history that there is a direct correlation between the quality of family life and the health of a people. In point of fact, however, these insights have always guided the Church's pastoral solicitude for families—even when not articulated in such dramatic fashion.

At times, our mental images of the Holy Family are nurtured more from pious holy cards than from reality. My own reflections are more often drawn to imagining poor Joseph. Being a husband and a father in "normal" circumstances is hard enough! He was additionally responsible for a virginal wife and a Divine Son. And yet, the Church insists that the home at Nazareth is indeed exemplary for all Christian homes. Why? Because it was never merely an arrangement of convenience. Because it was always a relationship rooted in God's will and law, thus bringing about a union of hearts. And that kind of human solidarity, precisely because it is grounded in Almighty God, can never be overcome by negative forces. This is one of the greatest glories of Gospel living and one of the greatest gifts that observant Christians can make to the societies in which they find themselves, as their personal experience of God's Kingdom in the family spreads into the culture at large.

The Church holds up for celebration, emulation, and veneration in a particular way the Holy Family of Nazareth on the Sunday within the Octave of Christmas. During Pope Paul VI's pastoral visit to Nazareth in 1965, he waxed eloquent on what he called the "School of Nazareth":

> I would like to return to my childhood and attend the simple yet profound school that is Nazareth! How wonderful to be close to Mary, learning again the lesson of the true meaning of life, learning again God's truths. But here we are only on pilgrimage. Time presses and I must set aside my desire to stay and carry on my education in the Gospel, for that education is never finished.[28]

It is interesting to note how Paul VI places Mary at the center of it all, perhaps recalling the insight of his venerable predecessor, Pius XII, who in an address to newlyweds in 1942 remarked:

> The mother is the sun of the family. She is its sun by her spirit of generosity and sacrifice, by her constant readiness, vigilance, delicacy and tact in all that touches the happiness of her husband and her children; she radiates light and warmth.... The wife is the sun of the family by the light of her smile and the warmth of her word.... The wife is the sun of the family by her natural frankness, by her straightforward dignity, by her irreproachable Christian behavior. She is its sun in the recollection and rectitude of spirit, in the subtle harmony of her bearing and dress, in her elegance and in her deportment—at once both reserved and affectionate.[29]

Mary, Mother of all mothers, by your holy example and powerful intercession, make all mothers to be the sun of their families.

∽

He took the substance of His human flesh from her, and clothed in it He lay within her; and He bore it about with Him after birth, as a sort of badge and witness that He, though God, was hers. He was nursed and tended by her; He was suckled by her; He lay in her arms. As time went on, He ministered to her, and obeyed her. He lived with her for thirty years, in one house, with an uninterrupted intercourse, and with only the saintly Joseph to share it with Him. She was the witness of His growth, of His joys, of His sorrows, of His prayers; she was blest with His smile, with the touch of His hand, with the whisper of His affection, with the expression of His thoughts and His feelings, for that length of time. Now, my brethren, what ought she to be, what is it becoming *that she should be, who was so favoured?*[30]

THE WEDDING FEAST AT CANA

Throughout the New Testament one finds references to Mary, especially at the most critical junctures in the life and ministry of her Son. Three passages of Johannine origin must be considered in some depth, as we come upon those scenes in our Marian journey.

Most serious Scripture commentators agree that John has the most highly developed theology and literary style of all the New Testament writers. The structure of John's Gospel is a masterpiece by which even the arrangement of material or the introduction of certain people advances the theological agenda of the Evangelist. For example, the unnamed "beloved disciple" is commonly accepted to be John himself—but is also generally regarded as a symbol for the ideal Christian in every age who stands with Jesus to the end, and beyond. Another figure of prominence is the Mother of the Lord, who appears only twice. Her appearances are at the beginning and the end of her Son's public ministry, as the Evangelist used the Hebraic device of "inclusion" to frame the Lord's earthly career.

It is interesting that John, who has no infancy narrative, does feel compelled to place Mary in the midst of events. He shows her to be the one responsible for Christ's "first sign" (John's preference, rather than "miracle"), when He responded to her firm faith, although He had already told her rather succinctly: "My hour has not yet come" (John 2:4). Jesus' responsiveness to His Mother in this passage has provided Christians throughout the ages with a sure basis for seeking Mary's intercession on their behalf.

～ঔ৩

It may be added, that, though, if sanctity was wanting, it availed nothing for influence with Our Lord, to be one of His company, still, as the Gospel shows, He on various occasions actually did allow those who were near Him, to be the channels of introducing supplicants to Him or of gaining miracles from Him, as in the instance of the miracle of the loaves; and if on one occasion, He seems to repel His Mother, when she told Him that wine was wanting for the guests at the marriage feast, it is obvious to remark on it, that, by saying that she was then separated from Him ("What have I to do with thee?") because His hour was not yet come, He implied, that when that hour was come, such separation would be at an end. Moreover, in fact He did at her intercession work the miracle to which her words pointed.

I consider it impossible then, for those who believe the Church to be one vast body in Heaven and on earth, in which every holy creature of God has his place, and of which prayer is the life, when once they recognize the sanctity and dignity of the Blessed Virgin, not to perceive immediately, that her office above is one of perpetual intercession for the faithful militant, and that our very relation to her must be that of clients to a patron, and that, in the eternal enmity which exists between the woman and the serpent, while the serpent's strength lies in being the Tempter, the weapon of the Second Eve and Mother of God is prayer.

As then these ideas of her sanctity and dignity gradually penetrated the mind of Christendom, so did that of her intercessory power follow close upon them and with them. From the earliest times that mediation is symbolized in those representations of her with uplifted hands, which, whether in plaster or in glass, are still extant in Rome—that Church, as St. Irenaeus says, with which "every Church, that is, the faithful from every side, must agree, because of its more powerful principality"; "into which," as Tertullian adds, "the Apostles poured out, together with their blood, their whole doctrine."[31]

MARY WITH JESUS PREACHING

As I imagine Our Lady amidst a crowd listening to her Son preach, I think of my own mother and her reactions to a similar situation two millennia later. The first was an obvious maternal pride: "Look at how people listen to my son!" On not a few occasions, my mother would also express concern: "I liked what you said, but I noticed some people seemed a bit annoyed. Be careful!"

Knowing her Son, Mary was able to lead others into an attitude of confidence in His regard. We can say that Jesus' signs were sermons in action. Thus, at Cana, she was able to instruct the waiters, "Do whatever He tells you" (John 2:5), knowing in advance what the result would be. Significantly, St. John says that after that first sign performed by the Lord, His disciples began to believe in Him (2:11). John doesn't say that about Mary. Why? Because she did not need that sign (or any other) to believe in Him; in point of fact, she knew Him so well that she actually facilitated the working of His first sign for the benefit of those who did not know Him yet in that way. And so, how her mother's heart must have swelled with pride when she would hear people say, "He has done all things well" (Mark 7:37).

On the other hand, when the gentle Jesus assumed the prophetic mantle, as all faithful preachers need to do from time to time, castigating hypocrisy and self-righteousness and pointing the finger at the offenders, how that maternal heart must have sunk in fear for her "boy." Can't we hear her plead, "Please, Son, You've said such things to me in the privacy of our home. Do You really have to say them in public, placing Yourself in jeopardy?" And can't we hear Him repeat, perhaps for the hundredth time, that retort He first uttered at the age of twelve: "Did you not know I had to be in My Father's house?" (Luke 2:49).

⚮

He vouchsafed to speak face to face [to Moses].... This was the great privilege of the inspired Lawgiver of the Jews; but how much was it below that of Mary! Moses had the privilege only now and then, from time to time; but Mary for thirty continuous years saw and heard Him, being all through that time face to face with Him, and being able to ask Him any question which she wished explained, and knowing that the answers she received were from the Eternal God, Who neither deceives nor can be deceived.[32]

THE *VIA CRUCIS*

Mothers always say how much they suffer in seeing their children suffer. How often we hear mothers say, with no exaggeration, "Would that *I* could have suffered that pain, instead of my child." The Church has always understood that sentiment and so, for centuries, has encouraged her children to make the *Via Crucis*, or Stations of the Cross. accompanied by the haunting chant of the

Stabat Mater, which is a reflection on the passion of the Lord from the perspective of His Mother.

Almost every viewer of Mel Gibson's *The Passion of the Christ* says the most poignant, heart-wrenching scene in the film is the meeting of Mother and Son along the road to Calvary: Their eyes meet. Words fail and are, in truth, inadequate to the need as they communicate from the depth of their souls—she in sorrow for Him, and He for her.

St. Alphonsus Liguori also captures the reality:

> Consider how the Son met His Mother on His way to Calvary. Jesus and Mary gazed at each other and their looks became as so many arrows to wound those hearts which loved each other so tenderly.[33]

And so that awareness should bring us to a deep spirit of compunction, St. Alphonsus prays:

> My most loving Jesus, by the pain You suffered in this meeting, grant me the grace of being truly devoted to Your most holy Mother. And You, my Queen, who were overwhelmed with sorrow, obtain for me by Your prayers a tender and a lasting remembrance of the passion of Your divine Son. I love You, Jesus, my Love, above all things. I repent of ever having offended You. Never allow me to offend You again. Grant that I may love You always; and then do with me as You will.[34]

❧

Jesus rises, though wounded by His fall, journeys on, with His Cross still on His shoulders. He is bent down; but at one place, looking up, He sees His Mother. For an instant they just see each other, and He goes forward.

Mary would rather have had all His sufferings herself, could that have been, than not have known what they were by ceasing to be near Him. He, too, gained a refreshment, as from some soothing and grateful breath of air, to see her sad smile amid the sights and the noises which were about Him. She had known Him beautiful and glorious, with the freshness of divine innocence and peace upon His countenance; now she saw Him so changed and deformed that she could scarce have recognized Him, save for the piercing, thrilling, peace-inspiring look He gave her. Still, He was now carrying the load of the world's sins, and, all-holy though He was, He carried the image of them on His very face. He looked like some outcast or outlaw who had frightful guilt upon Him. He had been made sin for us, Who knew no sin; not a feature, not a limb, but spoke of guilt, of a curse, of punishment, of agony.

Oh, what a meeting of Son and Mother! Yet there was a mutual comfort, for there was a mutual sympathy. Jesus and Mary—do they forget that Passiontide through all eternity?[35]

CALVARY

Bible-believing Christians must accept the doctrine of the Lord's virginal conception, but some balk at the notion of Mary's perpetual virginity (although their Protestant forebears—like Luther, Calvin, and Zwingli—all held firmly to that teaching). While there is no explicit New Testament text for Mary's perpetual virginity, the Church, of course, has never taken all her wisdom exclusively from Sacred Scripture. However, Jesus' entrustment of His Mother to the care of St. John offers us an intelligent clue: If the Blessed Mother did have other children, as some non-Catholic Christians assert (relying on Gospel texts that speak of Jesus' "brothers and sisters"), why would Jesus have acted thus? Why would Our Lord be concerned to commit His Mother to the care of St. John? Even more to the point, would Jesus' "brothers and sisters" have tolerated their Mother being given into the care of someone outside the family? Clearly, these "brothers and sisters" of the Lord are not children of the same mother but close relatives, who, to this day in the Middle East, are termed "brothers and sisters."

Beyond that very practical issue, there is also a powerful spiritual and theological truth conveyed in this episode.

The Lord's earthly ministry ended on Calvary, with the Beloved Disciple and Mary brought into a unique relationship with each other by the dying Christ. The Beloved Disciple, representative of every committed Christian, in that moment was given the Mother of Christ to be his own Mother. The physical maternity of Mary was thus extended and expanded to include now a spiritual motherhood of the Church, her Son's brothers and sisters. Just as she brought Christ's physical Body into the world, now she would play a role on behalf of His mystical Body (the Church). Mary did not ask for the role, nor did the Church give it to her; it was nothing less than her Divine Son's dying wish for her and for His Church (John 19:26).

It is significant that the Evangelist informs us that Jesus utters *"consummatum est"* ("It is finished, consummated, fulfilled") only after His Mother and the Beloved Disciple have been brought into that loving union of mother and son. In other words, claiming the Mother of the Lord as our Mother is not an optional add-on to Christian theology; it is essential.

❧

Mary is only our mother by divine appointment, given us from the Cross; her presence is above, not on earth; her office is external, not within us. Her name is not heard in the administration of the sacraments. Her work is not one of ministration towards us; her power is indirect. It is her prayers that avail, and her prayers are effectual by the fiat of Him who is our all in all. Nor need she hear us by any innate power, or any personal gift; but by His manifestation to her of the

52

prayers which we make to her. When Moses was on the Mount, the Almighty told him of the idolatry of his people at the foot of it, in order that he might intercede for them; and thus it is the Divine Presence which is the intermediating Power by which we reach her and she reaches us.[36]

THE CRUCIFIXION

Mothers don't expect to witness the deaths of their children, let alone their execution, particularly of one they know to be innocent. Imagine Mary, then, as she beheld the immolation of the innocent Lamb of God. That notion is highlighted by St. John, who observes that at the very hour of the Lord's death, the lambs were being slaughtered in the Temple.

When this Son of hers was but forty days old, the venerable Simeon prophesied that a sword would pierce her heart (Luke 2:35). Without a doubt, that chilling prophecy reverberated in her ears that first Good Friday afternoon. From the first moment of her Divine Son's existence in her virginal womb, Mary's life was an endless *fiat*. Accustomed to saying "yes" to the Father's will, she said it one last time as she united her mental anguish to Christ's torments.

Present with her and offering her human consolation was the Beloved Disciple. The two of them flanking the dying Lord form the rood screens of so many churches, especially in the English countryside. High up in the transept, they mark off the Holy of Holies, where the sacrifice of the Lamb of God is mystically and sacramentally re-presented.

The rood screen also provides a visual image of the virginal Church in the persons of the three virgins—Jesus, Mary, John— who form the *ecclesiola*, which is the infant Church born from the wounded side of Christ. The Church, like Mary, is that virginal mother who brings forth new life from that spotless womb of hers that is the baptismal font. The Church, like Mary, is that witness to the Lord's saving death as she faithfully proclaims her undying faith in His glorious Resurrection.

⧼❧

But great as was St. Paul's devotion to Our Lord, much greater was that of the Blessed Virgin; because she was His Mother, and because she had Him and all His sufferings actually before her eyes, and because she had the long intimacy of thirty years with Him, and because she was from her special sanctity so ineffably near to Him in spirit. When, then, He was mocked, bruised, scourged, and nailed to the Cross, she felt as keenly as if every indignity and torture inflicted on Him was struck at herself. She could have cried out in agony at every pang of His. This is called her compassion, or her suffering with her Son, and it arose from this that she was the "Vas insigne devotionis" [the "singular vessel of devotion"]. [37]

PENTECOST

St. Luke makes a point of noting Our Lady's presence among the disciples during that first novena to the Holy Spirit as the infant Church awaited the outpouring of Pentecostal power (Acts 1:14). Pope Benedict XVI "connects the dots" for us:

> It is the time of awaiting the Holy Spirit who came down on the nascent Church powerfully at Pentecost. The Church's tradition of dedicating the month of May to the Virgin Mary harmonizes very well with both

these contexts, the natural and the liturgical....At the same time, she is the humble and discreet protagonist of the first steps taken by the Christian community: Mary is its spiritual heart since her very presence among the disciples is a living memory of the Lord Jesus and a pledge of the gift of His Spirit.[38]

All of Mary's greatness as a Christian can be traced to the fact that the Holy Spirit came upon her, and that she lived in the presence of God, continuously aware of His Presence in her life. Our Lady cooperated with the Spirit's promptings and lived in loving obedience to God's Word, always saying "yes" to God. Mary the Virgin heeded the Lord's plan for her, and she became fruitful. Her life was an ongoing hymn of praise to the Father; she was a woman of peace and joy because she gave the Spirit of God free rein in her life. When Mary first received the Spirit into her heart, she did not keep Him to herself; she immediately went forth to share that experience and its meaning with others. She also realized that a life in the Spirit involves service to others; therefore, not considering her own precarious situation, she went through the rough hill country to tend to the needs of her elderly cousin Elizabeth.

What does all this have to do with us? A great deal, for what happened in the life of Mary can and must happen in our own lives. Each of us has received the Holy Spirit in Baptism and Confirmation, but have we done anything with the Spirit? Are we more peaceful, loving, or joyous for having received those sacraments? If not, we can say, paraphrasing Shakespeare, that the fault is not in the sacraments but in ourselves, that we have not activated the power of the Spirit in our lives. On Pentecost, the birthday of the Church, we look at the first and greatest Christian who ever lived, knowing that what the Spirit did for Mary, He will do only too gladly for us. Being a Spirit-filled person means bringing forth the fruits of the Spirit. Jesus said, "Thus you will know them by their fruits" (Matt 7:20). We know the fruit Mary brought forth, for every day we say: "Blessed is the fruit of thy womb, Jesus."

Am I possessed by God's Spirit? Another way of asking that same question is: Have I brought forth Christ to the world in which I live?

May…belongs to the Easter season, which lasts fifty days, and in that season the whole of May commonly falls, and the first half always. The great Feast of the Ascension of Our Lord into Heaven is always in May, except once or twice in forty years. Pentecost, called also Whit-Sunday, the Feast of the Holy Ghost, is commonly in May, and the Feasts of the Holy Trinity and Corpus Christi are in May not unfrequently. May, therefore, is the time in which there are such frequent Alleluias, because Christ has risen from the grave, Christ has ascended on high, and God the Holy Ghost has come down to take His place.

Here then we have a reason why May is dedicated to the Blessed Mary. She is the first of creatures, the most acceptable child of God, the dearest and nearest to Him. It is fitting then that this month should be hers, in which we especially glory and rejoice in His great Providence to us, in our redemption and sanctification in God the Father, God the Son, and God the Holy Ghost.[39]

MARY AND JOHN SHARE A HOME

We know from the Fourth Gospel that the Lord's dying wish was that His holy Mother and the Beloved Disciple would be bound together in a relationship of intimacy and devotion. Very tersely, the Evangelist remarks, "And from that hour the disciple took her to his own home" (John 19:27). The original Greek says that John took

Mary "*eis ta idia,*" not an easy phrase to translate, but quite suggestive. Literally, it means that he took her into his own affairs; we might say that he "made room for her in his life" or made her life a part of his. In this sense, the Beloved Disciple's response is paradigmatic for anyone who wants to be a "beloved disciple," so in accord with Christ's desire, that person must make room for Mary in his life of faith. That said, we know from the earliest Christian sources that John also took the Blessed Mother to live with him.

While we have moral certitude that Mary and John lived together, that's where the assuredness ends. One tradition has them dwelling in Ephesus, another on the island of Patmos, yet another in both places. The competing sites make compelling arguments for their particular location. But when all is said and done, we probably have to content ourselves with saying we really don't know the spot. What *does* matter, though, is that John was faithful to the Dying Lord's last request and that John reaped a great reward as a result.

Imagine living for years with the Mother of the Word Incarnate! What insights into the Person of the God-Man did the Evangelist gain as his holy curiosity probed the depths of Mary's mind and heart and she responded day after day not only with a mother's devotion but with the wisdom that comes from being the Seat of Wisdom and the Spouse of the Holy Spirit. No wonder that the Gospel of John is such a jewel of theology—a diamond revealing the many facets of the mystery of Christ. John's meditation and reflection on the Word-made-Flesh occurred in the School of Mary, and we have every reason to believe that all Christian disciples who also allow themselves to be tutored by Our Lady will be led to know her Divine Son in the most intimate and personal way.

❧

After He had left this earth, she had her duties towards the Apostles, and especially towards the Evangelists. She had duties towards the martyrs, and to the confessors in prison; to the sick, to the ignorant, and to the poor.

Afterwards, she had to seek with St. John another and a heathen country, where her happy death took place. But before that death, how much must she have suffered in her life amid an idolatrous population! Doubtless the angels screened her eyes from the worst crimes there committed. Still, she was full of duties there—and in consequence she was full of merit. All her acts were perfect, all were the best that could be done. Now, always to be awake, guarded, fervent, so as to be able to act not only without sin, but in the best possible way, in the varying circumstances of each day, denotes a life of untiring mindfulness. But of such a life, prudence is the presiding virtue. It is, then, through the pains and sorrows of her earthly pilgrimage that we are able to invoke her as the Virgo prudentissima.[40]

The Death of Mary

Throughout Christian history, two schools of thought have presented opposing views about the end of Our Lady's life here on Earth. The first maintains that she never died but was simply escorted by angels, body and soul, into Heaven. The second holds that she did indeed die, but that her body and soul were immediately reunited and brought to heavenly glory.

The proponents of the first position believe as they do because they argue that the Immaculate Virgin, whom no stain of any sin (original or actual) ever touched, would not have undergone the experience of death since death is a direct consequence of the sin of Adam. And so, it would be worthwhile to return to the third chapter of the Book of Genesis for a clearer understanding of the connection between that original sin and death.

Perhaps it would be helpful to consider the issue from a different but related issue. In the very same verse wherein God tells Adam that he is dust, and to dust he will return (Gen 3:19), we read about another punishment meted out to Adam (and presumably to his progeny), namely, that he shall have to earn his sustenance "by the sweat of his brow." Most of us have been conditioned from childhood to understand that statement to mean that because Adam sinned, he (and we) have to work, whereas that was not the case prior to his fall from grace. However, the biblical text does not say that. Indeed, Genesis 2:5 records the divine intention to create man, precisely with a view to his tilling of the soil and clearly in advance of the original sin. No, the punishment is not that human beings will have to work but that their work will be perceived as burdensome, tedious, and very often unfulfilling. Similarly, one can say that another penalty leveled against Adam is not that he and his descendants would die, but that he and they would experience death as fearsome and wrenching.

One can make the case that death is the most natural part of being a limited, finite human being. Without the original sin, one could argue, human beings might have died but viewed it as a normal, natural part of their existence, with a peaceful transition to the next life. And thus can the death of Our Lady be understood. To be sure, the Church has no definitive teaching on the matter; even the Venerable Pius XII in his dogmatic definition of the Assumption (*Munificentissimus Deus*, 1950) chose not to weigh in on either side of the discussion, allowing personal piety to hold sway. Thus, instead of writing "after Mary died," he wrote "when the course of her earthly life was finished"—which can be interpreted as implying Mary's death in the figurative language of sleep or as implying her immediate passage to Heaven without undergoing death. The *Catechism of the Catholic Church* likewise permits what we might term a "holy ambiguity" to prevail (*CCC* 966, 974).

Pope John Paul II, a "Marian" pope if ever there was one, nonetheless considered the physical death of Our Lady to be a suitable conformity to her Son, first of all, and in one of his many Marian catecheses, saw it as exemplary for us, too: "The experience of death personally enriched the Blessed Virgin: by undergoing mankind's common destiny, she can more effectively exercise her spiritual motherhood towards those approaching the last moment of their life."[41]

A proverb asserts that "as a man lives, so shall he die." The New Testament and our Catholic Faith assure us that the Blessed Virgin lived the holiest of lives, thus giving us the confidence that she also died the holiest of deaths, eager to rejoin her Son, face to face—an attitude which should be that of her children in the Church as well.

～

As soon as we apprehend by faith the great fundamental truth that Mary is the Mother of God, other wonderful truths follow in its train; and one of these is that she was exempt from the ordinary lot of mortals, which is not only to die, but to become earth to earth, ashes to ashes, dust to dust. Die she must, and die she did, as her Divine Son died, for He was man; but various reasons have approved themselves to holy writers, why, although her body was for a while separated from her soul and consigned to the tomb, yet it did not remain there, but was speedily united to her soul again, and raised by Our Lord to a new and eternal life of heavenly glory.

We are told by St. Matthew, that after Our Lord's death upon the Cross... "many bodies of the saints"—that is, the holy prophets, priests, and kings of former times—rose again in anticipation of the last day.

Can we suppose that Abraham, or David, or Isaias, or Ezechias, should have been thus favoured, and not God's own Mother? Had she not a claim on the love of her Son to have what any others had? Was she not nearer to Him than the greatest of the saints before her? And is it conceivable that the law of the grave should admit of relaxation in their case, and not in hers? Therefore we confidently say that Our Lord, having preserved her from sin and the consequences of sin by His Passion, lost no time in pouring out the full merits of that Passion upon her body as well as her soul.[42]

THE BURIAL OF MARY

A wonderful custom prevails in many quarters of the Church, especially in the Church's Eastern Rites, of blessing flowers on August 15, the Solemnity of Our Lady's Assumption into Heaven. What is the origin of that practice?

A first-century work attributed to St. Denis the Areopagite (*Books of Divine Names*) records a funeral panegyric delivered by one Hierotheus, who asserted that the apostles had been divinely warned of the impending death of the Virgin Mary. All except St. Thomas managed to return in time for her death and funeral. For three days, the apostles and other faithful maintained a vigil at her tomb, from which emanated at times the sound of heavenly music. When St. Thomas finally arrived, he asked to see the body of the Virgin Mary. To everyone's surprise, when the tomb was opened, her body was not there—only flowers and her burial shroud.

It seems that Thomas might have made a habit of not being around when he should have been. We recall that on the night of the Lord's first resurrection appearance to His disciples, Thomas was absent. After rejoining the confused and frightened band, he demanded some proof for their all-too-wonderful-to-believe declaration. A week later, the Risen Lord made another visitation and offered him the proof he requested. Thomas's skepticism actually gave Christ the opportunity to present a lesson on the nature of faith: "Blessed are those who have not seen and yet believe" (John 20:29). Lest we be too hasty in condemning the one who has been saddled with the moniker of "The Doubter," let us also remember that the strongest profession of faith in Jesus' divinity comes from the Doubter's lips: "My Lord and my God!" (John 20:28). As Cardinal Newman phrased it so aptly: "Ten thousand difficulties do not make one doubt, as I understand the subject; difficulty and doubt are incommensurate."[43]

If the pious legend is accurate, Thomas's absence and later insistence on seeing the body of the Blessed Virgin likewise gave Christians the knowledge that her body had not been subjected to the corruption of the grave—the fate of heirs to sin—but had been raised to that place prepared for her by her Divine Son.

⊱⊰

By her Assumption is meant that not only her soul, but her body also, was taken up to Heaven upon her death, so that there was no long period of her sleeping in the grave, as is the case with others, even great saints, who wait for the last day for the resurrection of their bodies.[44]

THE ASSUMPTION

The dogma of Mary's Assumption teaches that the Mother of the Lord was taken into Heaven, body and soul, since no decay should touch the body of her who bore the Messiah. Christians say they believe "in the resurrection of the body," and the doctrine of the Assumption merely asserts God's acknowledgment of Mary's worthiness to anticipate (from the earthbound perspective of human time) the fullness of salvation as both Mother of Christ and Mother of the Church. Here we see both a Christological and an ecclesiological dimension. The reward given to Mary is given ultimately in virtue of her divine maternity. It likewise points toward the resurrection of the dead, which is the hope of the whole Church.

Mary's privileges are promises. What God has done for her, He is willing to do for all the other members of His Son's Church. Mary's experience is unique only from the temporal point of view, in that the experience of salvation (her Immaculate Conception) and the experience of resurrection (her Assumption) are possible for all believers. In the most basic terms possible, the difference between Mary and the rest of the Church is that her possession of these gifts is present and real, while ours is an event of the future.

In the Risen Christ and the Assumed Virgin, both bodily present in Heaven, we behold the fullness of redeemed humanity—male and female, the New Adam and the New Eve—standing forth as signs of hope for all of us. Although the doctrine of Mary's bodily Assumption was believed by Christians from antiquity, it was only defined as a dogma by the Venerable Pope Pius XII in 1950, not creating a new teaching but proclaiming what had always been held from time immemorial. Perhaps the pontiff's reason, prompted by the Holy Spirit, was that modern man was in great need of hope, given the tragic wars of the twentieth century with their unspeakable assaults on human life and dignity. The Solemnity of the Assumption on August 15 is truly a celebration of hope reminding us that God does reward faithfulness. Mary's life of joyful service has been taken up into the risen life of Heaven. Like a good mother, she prays for us as she waits for us to reach the finish line. Like good children, we try to imitate her example, hoping to be found worthy of that eternal home where God is "all in all" (1 Cor 15:28).

For those Christians who find this dogma difficult to accept, I would offer two responses. First, if Elijah could be taken up to Heaven in a whirlwind, apparently without dying (2 Kings 2), why not the Mother of the Word Incarnate? Indeed, there is even a pious tradition among some Jews that Moses was also assumed into Heaven, hence the title of the Jewish apocryphal book *The Assumption of Moses* (or *The Testament of Moses*).

Second, as already pointed out, every Protestant Reformer accepted this event as self-evident. And so, to be true to one's Reformation roots would require one to share that same conviction. So meaningful a doctrine was this to Martin Luther that his burial chamber (in the Wittenberg church on whose door he had posted his ninety-five theses) was adorned with Peter Vischer's 1521 sculpture of the Coronation of the Virgin, with a Latin inscription for the feast of the Assumption. An English translation could be rendered thus: "The Queen, whose feast this is, is taken to her throne on high, escorted by the angelic choirs, and the Son Himself places His Mother in the high heavens." One would have to believe the sculpture and the inscription to be Luther's final words on the subject: Mary our Queen reigns gloriously in Heaven, by the express will of her Divine Son.

※

If her body was not taken into Heaven, where is it? how comes it that it is hidden from us? why do we not hear of her tomb as being here or there? why are not pilgrimages made to it? why are not relics producible of her, as of the saints in general? Is it not even a natural instinct which makes us reverent towards the places where our dead are buried? We bury our great men honourably. St. Peter speaks of the sepulchre of David as known in his day, though he had died many hundred years before. When Our Lord's body was taken down from the Cross, He was placed in an honourable tomb. Such too had been the honour already paid to St. John Baptist, his tomb being spoken of by St. Mark as generally known. Christians from the earliest times went from other countries to Jerusalem to see the holy places. And, when the time of persecution was over, they paid still more attention to the bodies of the saints, as of St. Stephen, St. Mark, St. Barnabas, St. Peter, St. Paul, and other Apostles and martyrs. These [bodies] were transported to great cities, and portions of them sent to this place or that. Thus, from the first to this day it has been a great feature and characteristic of the Church to be most tender and reverent towards the bodies of the saints. Now, if there was anyone who more than all would be preciously taken care of, it would be Our Lady. Why then do we hear nothing of the Blessed Virgin's body and its separate relics? Why is she thus the hidden Rose? Is it conceivable that they who had been so reverent and careful of the bodies of the saints and martyrs should neglect her—her who was the

Queen of Martyrs and the Queen of Saints, who was the very Mother of Our Lord? It is impossible. Why then is she thus the hidden Rose? Plainly because that sacred body is in Heaven, not on earth.[45]

QUEEN OF HEAVEN
AND
MOTHER OF THE CHURCH

The theme of the woman who is the Mother of the Church reaches a crescendo in Revelation 12. Even astute readers are brought up short as they try to unravel the symbolism. Is the woman laboring to give birth Mary or the Church? The author of Revelation was so skillful a writer that both interpretations are possible, and both were probably intended. Catholic theology sees the parallels as more than a happy coincidence, for the roles of Mary and the Church overlap or intersect at many points. This is apparent by the use of "inclusion" in the Gospel of John (with Our Lady introducing her Son to His public ministry at Cana and ending it with Him on Calvary) and is equally apparent in the Book of Revelation through the double symbolism employed by the sacred author.

Very wisely, then, does the Church select this passage as the First Reading for Holy Mass on the Solemnity of the Assumption, albeit a rather strange and highly symbolic passage that presents us with an image of Mary as the Mother of the Messiah, but equally the Mother of the Church. Mary had a dual role in the history of salvation. First, she was to be the instrument by which God entered human affairs in the flesh. Second, by her constant willingness to conduct her life according to God's plan and purpose, she indicated her suitability to be a member of the community of the redeemed established by Jesus as the Church. Mary, then, as the first Christian and surely the best, well deserves the title of Mother of the Church—that Church which is destined to be the Mystical Body of Christ spread out to every time and place.

Because she is that first and exemplary Christian that we know her to have been, the Church honors her by recalling the fact that Mary already shares in the fullness of redemption won for us all by her Son. While the rest of humanity must wait until the end of time to experience the resurrection of the body, Mary receives that privilege ahead of the rest of us. The first to say "yes" to God's plan is likewise the first to obtain the benefits brought about by that "yes."

⚬⚭⚬

One reason for believing in Our Lady's Assumption is that her Divine Son loved her too much to let her body remain in the grave. A second reason—that now before us—is this, that she was not only dear to the Lord as a mother is dear to a son, but also that she was so transcendently holy, so full, so overflowing with grace. Adam and Eve were created upright and sinless, and had a large measure of God's grace bestowed upon them; and, in consequence, their bodies would never have crumbled into dust, had they not sinned; upon which it was said to them, "Dust thou art, and unto dust thou shalt return." If Eve, the beautiful daughter of God, never would have become dust and ashes unless she had sinned, shall we not say that Mary, having never sinned, retained the gift which Eve by sinning lost? What had Mary done to forfeit the privilege given to our first parents in the beginning? Was her comeliness to be turned into corruption, and her fine gold to become dim, without reason assigned? Impossible. Therefore we believe that, though she died for a short hour, as did Our Lord Himself, yet, like Him, and by His almighty power, she was raised again from the grave.[46]

66

Mary in Catholic Devotion

MARIAN TITLES

In *Lumen Gentium* ("Dogmatic Constitution on the Church"), the Council Fathers of Vatican II teach us that the mystery of the Church is so great that no single image can capture its reality. Rather, the Church is like a multifaceted diamond that, when held up to the light at different angles, offers new and beautiful experiences. The Church has regarded the person of Mary in a similar way, resorting to numerous titles to help the faithful appreciate her. This is done in compelling fashion in the traditional Litany of Loreto (whose titles formed the basis of Cardinal Newman's daily meditations for the month of May, many of which grace our present volume). *Lumen Gentium* 62 also highlights numerous titles of the Blessed Virgin, and does it with great balance:

> This motherhood of Mary in the order of grace continues uninterruptedly from the consent which she loyally gave at the Annunciation and which she sustained without wavering beneath the cross, until the eternal fulfillment of all the elect. Taken up to Heaven she did not lay aside this saving office, but by her manifold intercession continues to bring us the gifts of eternal salvation. Therefore, the Blessed Virgin is invoked in the Church under the titles of Advocate, Helper, Benefactress, and Mediatrix.

The *Catechism of the Catholic Church* later used this same passage from *Lumen Gentium* to explain Mary's motherhood in relation to the Church (*CCC* 969).

The titles chosen by the Fathers of the Second Vatican Council underscore Mary's role as an intercessor on our behalf. At times, we

hear some of our "separated brethren" express disapproval of the
Catholic practice of seeking the intercession of the saints—although
they are not adverse to the practice of seeking the intercession of one
another in the present moment: "Would you please pray for me?" If
you and I can intercede for others (and we surely can), why not the
saints in glory? And why not the Queen of Saints, the Virgin Mother
of God? An invocation we learned in childhood makes eminently
good sense: "Pray for us, O holy Mother of God, that we may be
made worthy of the promises of Christ."

❧

*A tower in its simplest idea is a fabric for defence against enemies.
David, King of Israel, built for this purpose a notable tower; and as he
is a figure or type of Our Lord, so is his tower a figure denoting Our
Lord's Virgin Mother.*

*She is called the Tower of David because she had so signally ful-
filled the office of defending her Divine Son from the assaults of His foes.
It is customary with those who are not Catholics to fancy that the honours we pay to her interfere with the supreme worship which we pay to
Him; that in Catholic teaching she eclipses Him. But this is the very
reverse of the truth. For if Mary's glory is so very great, how cannot His
be greater still Who is the Lord and God of Mary? He is infinitely above
His Mother; and all that grace which filled her is but the overflowings
and superfluities of His incomprehensible sanctity. And history teaches
us the same lesson. Look at the Protestant countries which threw off all
devotion to her three centuries ago, under the notion that to put her from
their thoughts would be exalting the praises of her Son. Has that consequence really followed from their profane conduct towards her? Just the
reverse—the countries, Germany, Switzerland, England, which so
acted, have in great measure ceased to worship Him, and have given up
their belief in His Divinity while the Catholic Church, wherever she is
to be found, adores Christ as true God and true Man, as firmly as ever*

she did; and strange indeed would it be, if it ever happened otherwise. Thus Mary is the "Tower of David."[47]

MARY'S SEVEN SORROWS, OR DOLORS

The Church throughout the world celebrates the Triumph of the Cross on September 14, and the Roman Rite fittingly follows that up the very next day with its commemoration of Our Lady of Sorrows. Popular piety has identified seven "dolors" of the Blessed Virgin: the prophecy of Simeon; the flight into Egypt; the loss of the Boy Jesus; her meeting her Son on the way to Calvary; the death of Jesus on the Cross; her reception of her Son's dead body; and the placing of that body in the tomb. Only the most heartless, insensitive person would not be moved by that list of sorrowful events, as the hymn *Stabat Mater* plaintively demands our compassion:

> Who, on Christ's dear Mother gazing,
> Pierced by anguish so amazing,
> Born of woman, would not weep?
>
> Who, of Christ's dear Mother thinking,
> Such a cup of sorrow drinking,
> Would not share her sorrows deep?

At the same time, one might be moved to ask how one can experience such bitterness without becoming bitter. The answer lies in the development of compassion, which comes from the Latin word for "suffering with" another. Mary "suffered with" her Son and endeavored to cultivate the same attitudes as He: total abandonment to the will of the Father; unreserved love for a world in need of salvation; a desire to heal and make whole; a willingness to be a victim on behalf of those who did not even know they needed saving. Thus, the union of minds and hearts of Jesus and Mary resulted in a union of suffering—compassion. This is no cheap "tea and sympathy" approach to life; it is the very essence of what it means to be completely with and for the other. Our Lady epitomized compassion, rendered not only to her Son but even now to all her Son's brothers and sisters in the Church, of which she is—by God's design—the compassionate Mother.

ॐ

St. Paul calls elect souls vessels of honour: of honour, because they are elect or chosen; and vessels, because, through the love of God, they are filled with God's heavenly and holy grace. How much more then is Mary a vessel of honour by reason of her having within her, not only the grace of God, but the very Son of God, formed as regards His flesh and blood out of her!

But He, Who bore the sinner's shame for sinners, spared His Mother, who was sinless, this supreme indignity. Not in the body, but in the soul, she suffered. True, in His agony she was agonised; in His passion she suffered a fellow passion; she was crucified with Him; the spear that pierced His breast pierced through her spirit. Yet there were no visible signs of this intimate martyrdom; she stood up, still, collected, motionless, solitary, under the cross of her Son, surrounded by angels, and shrouded in her virginal sanctity from the notice of all who were taking part in His crucifixion.[48]

THE SEVEN SENTENCES OF MARY

To a culture like ours, awash in words (most of them meaningless), the Holy House of Nazareth probably would have been a most uncomfortable place because it seems to have been an abode pervaded by holy silence. Since not a single word of the Lord's foster father is recorded in Sacred Scripture, he has been dubbed "Joseph the Silent." It would appear that Our Lady might not have been that much more talkative, as we have only seven "words" or sentences of hers preserved in the Scriptures, perhaps paralleling in an interesting way her divine Son's seven last words proclaimed from the cross.

Mary's first two sentences occurred during the Annunciation (Luke 1:26–38) as first she sought to understand how she, a virgin, could become the Mother of the Messiah. Gabriel's word (which is really God's word) was sufficient for her to then exclaim, "Behold I am the handmaid of the Lord. Let it be to me according to your word." During her visit of charity and evangelization to Elizabeth, she then broke forth into her extended "word" of exultant praise of the God Who had done "great things" for her, so that "all generations to come" would call her "blessed" (Luke 1:46–55). Mary's *Magnificat* has served as the climax of the Church's evening prayer of Vespers for centuries and has likewise been the focus of hundreds of glorious musical settings throughout history.

The next time we hear a word from the Blessed Mother, it is truly a mother's word, spoken in frustration and relief as Mary and Joseph find their precocious Child among the rabbis in the Temple: "Why have you treated us so?" (Luke 2:48). The response of the Boy Jesus must have chastened her somewhat, for we do not hear from her again until the first day of the Lord's public ministry at Cana. She tells her Son, "They have no wine," and then gives the servants the only command of hers recorded in the New Testament: "Do whatever he tells you" (John 2:3, 5). From that moment forward, she becomes "Mary the Silent."

Of course, her counsel to the waiters at Cana is the best advice she ever could have given, not just to them, but to us as well. Having brought her Son to the moment of the revelation of His glory and having led His disciples to begin to believe in Him (John 2:11), she had fulfilled her role in salvation history. No more speaking was necessary, just maternal watching, waiting, and interceding, done in the hope that all her Son's brothers and sisters in His Church would follow her holy example.

❧

"But Mary kept all these things, and pondered them in her heart." (Luke ii:19)

Little is told us in Scripture concerning the Blessed Virgin, but there is one grace of which the Evangelists make her the pattern, in a few simple sentences—of faith. Zacharias questioned the Angel's message, but "Mary said, Behold the handmaid of the Lord; be it unto me according to thy word." Accordingly Elisabeth, speaking with an apparent allusion to the contrast thus exhibited between her own highly favoured husband, righteous Zacharias, and the still more highly favoured Mary, said, on receiving her salutation, "Blessed art thou among women, and blessed is the fruit of thy womb; Blessed is she that believed, for there shall be a performance of those things which were told her from the Lord."

But Mary's faith did not end in a mere acquiescence in Divine providences and revelations: as the text informs us, she "pondered" them. When the shepherds came, and told of the vision of angels which they had seen at the time of the Nativity, and how one of them announced that the Infant in her arms was "the Saviour, which is Christ the Lord," while others did but wonder, "Mary kept all these things, and pondered them in her heart." Again, when her Son and Saviour had come to the age of twelve years, and had left her for awhile for His Father's service, and had been found, to her surprise, in the Temple, amid the doctors, both hearing them and asking them questions, and had, on her addressing Him, vouchsafed to justify His conduct, we are told, "His mother kept all these sayings in her heart." And accordingly, at the marriage feast in Cana, her faith anticipated His first miracle, and she said to the servants, "Whatsoever he saith unto you, do it."

Thus St. Mary is our pattern of Faith, both in the reception and in the study of Divine Truth. She does not think it enough to accept, she dwells upon it; not enough to possess, she uses it; not enough to assent, she develops it; not enough to submit the Reason, she reasons upon it; not indeed reasoning first, and believing afterwards, with Zacharias, yet first believing without reasoning, next from love and reverence, reasoning after believing. And thus she symbolizes to us, not only the faith of the unlearned, but of the doctors of the Church also, who have to investigate, and weigh, and define, as well as to profess the Gospel; to draw the line between truth and heresy; to anticipate or remedy the various aberrations of wrong reason; to combat pride and recklessness with their own arms; and thus to triumph over the sophist and the innovator.[49]

THE MYSTERIES OF THE ROSARY

It is probably no exaggeration to suggest that when non-Catholics are asked to identify a specific form of prayer they associate with Catholics, it is the Rosary, which not infrequently accompanies Catholics even into eternity as their hands are wrapped in the beads in their coffin. The popes of every age have recommended this form of prayer, with Leo XIII penning eleven encyclicals on the Holy Rosary. Traditionally, the month of October is devoted in a special way to the recitation of the Rosary as the Church celebrates on October 7 the memorial of Our Lady of the Rosary, originally called Our Lady of Victory because of the totally unexpected and stunning victory of the greatly outnumbered Christian forces over those of the Muslims at the 1571 Battle of Lepanto—a victory Pope St. Pius V attributed to the fervent praying of the Rosary by all of Christendom.

The Rosary is a meditative form of prayer, combining elements of formulaic prayer (Our Father, Hail Mary, Glory Be) and reflection on the mysteries of redemption. It was originally intended to be the poor and illiterate man's Psalter, since the 150 Hail Marys parallel the 150 psalms. Catholics do not see in the Rosary the vain repetition of words that some non-Catholic Christians see, because we are not seeking to win a hearing by the sheer multiplication of words (Matt 6:7). On the contrary, the emphasis is not on the words but on the attitude and atmosphere of prayer that is created, allowing the believer to become lost in reflection on the divine and enabling us to hear God more clearly when He speaks.

Sometimes uninformed individuals attack the recitation of the Rosary as "Mariolatry." What must be understood is that the Rosary is, at root, a Christological prayer far more than a Marian one. Catholics pray to Our Lady and with her for the grace to meditate on the mysteries of our salvation with the same fervor as did she (Luke 2:51). Wisely and insightfully, Pope Paul VI in *Marialis Cultus* described the Rosary as "the compendium of the whole Gospel" (no. 42).

In 2002, Pope John Paul II issued his apostolic letter *Rosarium Virginis Mariae*, in which he announced a "Year of the Rosary" for 2002 to 2003, what he deemed a fitting homage to the Blessed Virgin as he embarked on the twenty-fifth anniversary of his election as the Successor of Peter. In that same document, the pope also offered the Church a fourth set of mysteries—the Luminous Mysteries, or Mysteries of Light—to join the traditional Joyful, Sorrowful, and Glorious Mysteries already in place for centuries. He ended his letter with these touching words:

> A prayer so easy and yet so rich truly deserves to be rediscovered by the Christian community. . . . Rediscover the Rosary in the light of Scripture, in harmony with the Liturgy, and in the context of your daily lives.
>
> May this appeal of mine not go unheard! (no. 43)

◈

This title of "Help of Christians" relates to those services of which the Divine Office, while recording and referring to the occasion on which it was given her,…connecting them more or less with the Rosary.

The first was on the first institution of the Devotion of the Rosary by St. Dominic, when, with the aid of the Blessed Virgin, he succeeded in arresting and overthrowing the formidable heresy of the Albigenses in the South of France.

The second was the great victory gained by the Christian fleet over the powerful Turkish Sultan, in answer to the intercession of Pope St. Pius V, and the prayers of the associations of the Rosary all over the Christian world…

The third was, in the words of the Divine Office, "the glorious victory won at Vienna, under the guardianship of the Blessed Virgin, over the most savage Sultan of the Turks, who was trampling on the necks of the Christians; in perpetual memory of which benefit Pope Innocent XI…dedicated the Sunday in the Octave of her Nativity as the feast of her august Name."

The fourth instance of her aid was the victory over the innumerable force of the same Turks in Hungary on the Feast of St. Mary ad Nives, in answer to the solemn supplication of the Confraternities of the Rosary.[50]

LOURDES, FATIMA, GUADALUPE

Some non-Catholic Christians express concern over Catholic involvement with visions or apparitions. While the Church is in fact extremely circumspect in accepting the validity of any new visions or apparitions, she also believes that "nothing is impossible with God" (Luke 1:37) and therefore does not reject the idea outright, as some Christians do. If God could reveal Himself or send intermediaries in both the Old and New Testaments (even after the Lord's Resurrection), why should this be out of the question today? Any apparitions approved by the Church (whether of Our Lord to St. Margaret Mary or of the Blessed Virgin at Lourdes or Fatima) have a remarkable similarity of theme; there is no new revelation but a restatement of the heart of the Gospel message: "Repent, and believe in the gospel!" (Mark 1:15). This is no more and no less than the message of most Bible-believing preachers.

What is the purpose of apparitions? One could say that they serve as wake-up calls from Heaven. The parable of the vinedresser (Matt 21:33–41) comes to mind in this regard. Jesus says that the owner of the vineyard repeatedly sends messengers who are ignored and even maltreated. The divine logic then concludes that they will heed the *alter ego* of the owner—his very own son. As God continues to call the world to conversion and then to maintenance in holiness, He offers myriad aids: the Church; the Sacred Scriptures; the sacraments; the example of holy people, both living and dead. But the witness of history is that all too often the world is tone-deaf to these divine overtures. And so, in the equivalent of a last-ditch attempt (humanly speaking), God makes new direct interventions in extraordinary ways, approaching humanity personally or through heavenly intermediaries (angels, Our Lady, other saints) and choosing individuals to receive His warnings (or consolations). These individuals, in turn, are obliged to share the message they have received with the rest of the Church or even the whole world. In the *Summa Theologiae*, St. Thomas Aquinas sums it up well: "Not indeed for the declaration of any new doctrine of faith, but for the direction of human acts."[51]

While the Church has a cautious attitude toward miracles and apparitions, it is good to realize that every modern pope has felt the need to make himself a "Marian pilgrim." After his election, Blessed John XXIII's first trip outside the Vatican was to the shrine of Our

Lady of Loreto. Pope John Paul II never missed an opportunity to visit a Marian sanctuary and there commend himself to Our Lady's maternal care. What they seemed to be saying by their actions is that, in their role as Successor of Peter and Vicar of Christ on Earth, they wanted to bring the whole Church to Mary, Mother of the Church, especially to those places she graced by her presence in a particular way. Thus, while blind, unthinking credulity of visions and apparitions is to be avoided at all costs, a coarse skepticism born of excessive rationalism should also be shunned. Here we are reminded of the wisdom of that line we find in the all-time favorite film *The Song of Bernadette*: "For those who believe in God, no explanation is necessary. For those who do not believe in God, no explanation is possible."

As a result of the appearance of the Blessed Mother at Guadalupe, human sacrifice ceased in Mexico and an entire people came into the communion of the Church. Lourdes is the best-known site of miraculous healings in history. The Virgin at Fatima issued a clarion call for repentance and reparation, which would provide the necessary conditions for world peace. In each instance, Our Lady assumed the prophetic mantle as God's spokeswoman and merely repeated her directive to the wine stewards at Cana: "Do whatever he tells you" (John 2:5).

❧

I recollect one saying among others of my confessor, a Jesuit Father, one of the holiest, most prudent men I ever knew. He said that we could not love the Blessed Virgin too much, if we loved Our Lord a great deal more.[52]

As then these ideas of her [Mary's] sanctity and dignity gradually penetrated the mind of Christendom, so did that of her intercessory power follow close upon them and with them.[53]

This simply is the point which I shall insist on—disputable indeed by aliens from the Church but most clear to her children, that the glories

of Mary are for the sake of Jesus; and that we praise and bless her as the
first of creatures, that we may duly confess Him as our sole Creator.[54]

LESSER-KNOWN APPARITIONS

While Guadalupe, Lourdes, and Fatima tend to be almost household names, many other apparitions have received ecclesiastical approval over the centuries: Knock (Ireland, 1789); Rue du Bac (France, 1830); LaSalette (France, 1846); Pontmain (France, 1871); Banneaux (Belgium, 1932); Beauraing (Belgium, 1932–33). Several common threads run through all valid apparitions: the seers are "common" folk; the heavenly interventions occur during times of crisis for the Church or the world; initial reactions are skeptical or even hostile, requiring a validating sign.

Why does God enable human beings to work miracles? asks St. Thomas Aquinas. Or why miraculous events? For two reasons, he says:

First and principally, in confirmation of the doctrine that a man teaches. For since those things which are of faith surpass human reason, they cannot be proved by human arguments, but need to be proved by the argument of divine power: so that when a man does works that God alone can do, we may believe that what he says is from God: just as when a man is the bearer of letters sealed with the king's ring, it is to be believed that what they contain expresses the king's will. ...[And the second purpose is] to make known God's presence in a man by the grace of the Holy Ghost: so that when a man does the works of God we may believe that God dwells in him by His grace.[55]

80

That said, Aquinas concedes that "miracles lessen the merit of faith," but—nonetheless—he declares, "it is better for them to be converted to the faith even by miracles than that they should remain altogether in their unbelief."[56]

Truth be told, the Church herself always exhibits a healthy skepticism when such extraordinary events are reported, with the presumption that the "seer" is either a deceiver or self-deceived. Clear criteria exist to test the veracity of the claim of supernatural character, among which are the orthodoxy of the message, the visionary's spirit of willing submission to ecclesiastical judgment, and good fruits flowing from the event. Investigations into visions are conducted at the local or diocesan level, through recourse to theologians, pastors, psychiatrists, and other professionals in a position to evaluate the spiritual and mental state of the seer. Some investigations result in relatively quick judgments, usually negative, while other investigations can go on for years and may yield an indeterminate decision. It has been estimated that for every alleged apparition the Church accepts, there are a hundred that never receive a favorable judgment.

Sometimes people ask, "What does it matter if a vision is really occurring or not, as long as good things are happening, for example, conversions, cures?" It matters a great deal because the act of faith must always be grounded in reality and truth; it can never be based on a falsehood. That is why the Evangelists went to great pains to convince their readers that the Lord's resurrection appearances were real and not phantasms; hence, the stress on His eating and drinking and being able to be touched. Belief is serious business, and God wants no one to be duped for He is, as the traditional Act of Faith prayer declares, the One Who "can neither deceive nor be deceived."

The present moment in history finds us confronted with hundreds of purported supernatural visitations. This proliferation is not cause for rejoicing. On the contrary, it suggests that people are not being spiritually fed through the normal means of grace, such as good catechesis and preaching, uplifting celebrations of the sacraments, and strong witnesses to Christian living. As a result, they feel compelled to chase after dubious substitutes. Jesus cautioned us against such a spirit: "An evil and adulterous generation seeks a sign." He continued: "But no sign shall be given it except the sign of Jonah the prophet" (Matt 12:39). Jonah's message was a call to repentance; his sign in the belly of the whale for three days and nights was a prefigurement of Christ's very passion, death, and resurrection. Time after time, the Blessed Virgin, Queen of Prophets, directs us toward the "sign of Jonah" as she urges repentance through reception of the sacrament of Penance and an experience of her Son's paschal mystery through a worthy and devout reception of the Holy Eucharist.

∽

But this is not all; in another respect we are really far more favoured than they were [those who witnessed biblical miracles]; they had outward miracles; we too have miracles, but they are not outward but inward. Ours are not miracles of evidence, but of power and influence. They are secret, and more wonderful and efficacious because secret. Their miracles were wrought upon external nature; the sun stood still, and the sea parted. Ours are invisible, and are exercised upon the soul. They consist in the sacraments, and they just do that very thing which the Jewish miracles did not. They really touch the heart, though we so often resist their influence. If then we sin, as, alas! we do, if we do not love God more than the Jews did, if we have no heart for those "good things which pass men's understanding," we are not more excusable than they, but less so. For the supernatural works which God showed to them were wrought outwardly, not inwardly, and did not influence the will; they did but convey warnings; but the supernatural works which He does towards us are in the heart, and impart grace; and if we disobey, we are not disobeying His command only, but resisting His presence.[57]

Catholics, then, hold the mystery of the Incarnation; and the Incarnation is the most stupendous event which ever can take place on earth; and after it and henceforth, I do not see how we can scruple at any miracle on the mere ground of its being unlikely to happen. No miracle can be so great as that which took place in the Holy House of Nazareth; it is indefinitely more difficult to believe than all the miracles of the Breviary, of the Martyrology, of saints' lives, of legends, of local traditions, put together; and there is the grossest inconsistency on the very face of the matter, for anyone so to strain out the gnat and to swallow the camel, as to profess what is inconceivable, yet to protest against what is surely within the limits of intelligible hypothesis. If, through divine grace, we once are able to accept the solemn truth that the Supreme Being was born of a mortal woman, what is there to be imagined which can offend us on the ground of its marvellousness?[58]

Marian Flowers

Many of us can recall with some nostalgia the de rigeur hymn for May crownings during our childhood years and apparently once more in fashion:

> Bring flow'rs of the fairest,
> Bring flow'rs of the rarest,
> From garden and woodland
> And hillside and vale;
> Our full hearts are swelling,
> Our glad voices telling
> The praise of the loveliest
> Rose of the vale.

What Mary Means to Christians

Flowers, "bringing in the May," and Mary seem to have been closely connected for centuries, at least in the northern hemisphere. In these climes, May heralds the definitive arrival of spring, with myriad plants blossoming forth in new life. And when a Christian thinks of new life, he instinctively thinks of Christ and then Mary, from whom Christ received the gift of life.

Traditional Christian piety has always enlisted nature in its praise of God, seen in an impressive way in the glorious *Exsultet* of the Easter Vigil, wherein the cantor calls on "all creation" to join the Church in her jubilant praise of the Risen Lord—even the bees who produced the honey to make the paschal candle! As believers have reflected on the beauty of creation throughout the ages, they have also found in various physical things reminders of spiritual realities; that has been particularly true of flowers and Mary, so that the thirteenth-century German poet Konrad Würzburg could hail the Virgin with these lines: "You are a living paradise / Of gloriously colored flowers." It may surprise some to learn that over seventy-five species of flowers have Marian names or associations, although many others lost such titles after the Protestant Reformation.

The lowly violet, long associated with humility, came to be known as Our Lady's Modesty, from the belief that it blossomed when Mary responded to Gabriel with her *fiat*: "Behold I am the handmaid of the Lord; let it be to me according to your word" (Luke 2:38). The snowdrop has been viewed as a symbol of Mary's purity and is called the Flower of the Purification since it is believed to have bloomed on February 2, the feast of the Infant Jesus' Presentation in the Temple, but also the feast of Mary's Purification.

Several flowers seem to have elicited thoughts about the flight into Egypt. One legend holds that on that journey, a band of robbers accosted the Holy Family and took Mary's purse, only to discover upon opening it that marigolds fell out rather than coins. Sicilian lore says that as Herod's soldiers pursued the Holy Family, the plant known as the Madonna's Juniper Bush opened its branches to shelter them, while the rosemary bush is credited with providing them shelter during the flight itself. Since holy people—like God Himself—are never outdone in generosity, the rosemary and lavender (also known as Mary's Drying Plant) were thought to have gotten their fragrance from the linens Our Lady hung on their branches to dry—an act of gratitude from the Holy Virgin Mother for the use of their boughs. Sea-pink or thrift was credited with forming cushions for Mary when she rested along that tiresome journey.

Our Lady's Thistle got its name from the belief that its spots were drops of milk that fell on them as Mary nursed her Son. The strawberry was also called the Fruitful Virgin due to a popular belief that Our Lady would take the Child Jesus "a-berrying" on the feast of the birth of John the Baptist, the Lord's cousin and precursor. The blue wood hyacinth got named Our Lady's Thimble since weaving and sewing were thought to have been the means by which Mary made a living for the family. A charming story relates that the young Jesus hung the pendant blossoms of the fuchsia (also the impatiens plant) on His Mother's ears, thus earning it the nickname of Our Lady's Eardrop. The foxglove plant is known in France as *Gant de Notre Dame* (Our Lady's Glove). The lily of the valley, also known as Mary's Tears, got its name from the belief that as Our Lady wept at the foot of the cross, her tears turned into this flower.

It is interesting to note that so many of these Marian flowers got their names in England, whose own pre-Reformation title was "Mary's Dowry," which realization has caused many to pray and hope that Our Lady would also serve as the Mother of Unity, bringing her "dowry" back into full communion with her Son's Church under Peter's successor.

The refrain of that beautiful May-crowning hymn brings together the themes we have been considering:

O Mary! we crown thee with blossoms today,
Queen of the Angels, Queen of the May.
O Mary! we crown thee with blossoms today,
Queen of the Angels, Queen of the May.

❦

I begin by making a distinction which will go far to remove good part of the difficulty of my undertaking, as it presents itself to ordinary inquirers,—the distinction between faith and devotion. I fully grant that devotion towards the Blessed Virgin has increased among Catholics with the progress of centuries; I do not allow that the doctrine concerning her has undergone a growth, for I believe that it has been in substance one and the same from the beginning.[59]

THE ROSE—
QUEEN OF THE FLOWERS

I suspect that everyone considers the rose the "queen of flowers." In almost every culture, the rose has held quasi-mystical value. In the Greco-Roman world, the rose symbolized beauty, love, and the season of spring; it also denoted the fragility of beauty and hinted at death, so that the pagan Roman feast of *rosalia* was a celebration of the dead. In Christian iconography, the rose came to stand for an eternal paradise, as well as being the symbol for martyrs. Not surprisingly, then, the rose has been considered the quintessential botanical representation of the Blessed Virgin Mary.

What Advent is complete without singing "Lo, How a Rose E'er Blooming"? The rose spoken of there is Christ Himself. However, if Christ has a human nature, He received it from His holy Mother, who must likewise be a rose since like always comes from like. Surely, that was Dante's understanding as we hear Beatrice counsel Dante in the *Paradiso*:

> Why are you so enamored of my face
> that you do not turn your gaze
> to the beautiful garden which blossoms
> under the radiance of Christ? There is the rose
> in which the Divine Word became flesh;
> here are the lilies whose perfume
> guides you in the right ways. (23:71–75)

And so, we sing:

> Lo, how a Rose e'er blooming
> from tender stem hath sprung!
> Of Jesse's lineage coming,
> as men of old have sung.
> It came, a floweret bright,
> amid the cold of winter,
> when half-spent was the night.
>
> Isaiah 'twas foretold it,
> the Rose I have in mind;
> with Mary we behold it,
> the Virgin Mother kind.
> To show God's love aright,
> she bore to us a Savior,
> when half-spent was the night.

According to the anonymous medieval author of these verses, Jesus the Rose has come forth from that "tender stem" who is Mary. The hymnographer proceeds to teach us that we see the Son best through the lens provided by the kindly Mother, who brings us the

Savior to demonstrate the depths of divine love. And this provides us with yet another Marian title—Mother of Fair Love. The rose once more betokens love.

In splendid Gothic cathedrals, our attention is drawn to the magnificent rose windows, with the central one depicting Mary presenting the Infant to the world, as she has ever done since that midnight in Bethlehem. Likewise, in the Middle Ages under the influence of courtly manners and culture, the rose garden came to be regarded as the privileged place to encounter one's beloved lady. Spiritualizing that notion, especially in light of the Song of Songs, led to the rose being viewed as the mystical union between the soul and Christ, between Christ and the Church, with Mary as the primordial example of such a blessed relationship, so that the Litany of Loreto could invoke her as "Mystical Rose."

Roses also began to represent those prayers, especially the *Aves* offered to Mary in that meditative prayer eventually called a "rosary," that is, a collection of roses. Some rosary beads are actually made in the form of roses to reinforce the meaning.

Shakespeare would opine in *Romeo and Juliet*: "A rose by any other name would smell as sweet." Pope Benedict XVI asserts: "Indeed, she is the most beautiful flower to have unfolded since the Creation, the 'rose' that appeared in the fullness of time when God, by sending His Son, gave the world a new springtime."[60] And so, we would have to part company with the Bard of Avon on that one, for the sweetest-smelling rose has the name of Mary.

❧

How did Mary become the Rosa Mystica, the choice, delicate, perfect flower of God's spiritual creation? It was by being born, nurtured and sheltered in the mystical garden or Paradise of God. Scripture makes use of the figure of a garden, when it would speak of Heaven and its blessed inhabitants. A garden is a spot of ground set apart for trees and plants, all good, all various, for things that are sweet to the taste or fragrant in scent, or beautiful to look upon, or useful for nourishment; and accordingly in its spiritual sense it means the home of blessed spirits and holy souls dwelling there together, souls with both the flowers and the fruits upon them, which by the careful husbandry of God they have come to bear, flowers and fruits of grace, flowers more beautiful and more fragrant than those of any garden, fruits more delicious and exquisite than can be matured by earthly husbandman....

Thus our first parents were placed in "a garden of pleasure" shaded by trees, "fair to behold and pleasant to eat of," with the Tree of Life in the midst, and a river to water the ground. Thus Our Lord, speaking from the Cross to the penitent robber, calls the blessed place, the Heaven to which He was taking him, "paradise," or a garden of pleasure. Therefore St. John, in the Apocalypse, speaks of Heaven, the palace of God, as a garden or paradise, in which was the Tree of Life giving forth its fruits every month.[61]

Appendices

THE MYSTERIES OF THE ROSARY

Joyful Mysteries

    1. The Annunciation
    2. The Visitation
    3. The Nativity of Our Lord
    4. The Presentation of Jesus in the Temple
    5. The Finding of the Child Jesus in the Temple

Luminous Mysteries*

    1. The Baptism of Jesus in the Jordan
    2. The Wedding Feast at Cana
    3. Jesus' Proclamation of the Kingdom of God
    4. The Transfiguration
    5. The Institution of the Eucharist

Sorrowful Mysteries

    1. The Agony in the Garden
    2. The Scourging at the Pillar
    3. The Crowning with Thorns
    4. The Carrying of the Cross
    5. The Crucifixion

---

* Instituted by Pope John Paul II as optional in his apostolic letter *Rosarium Virginis Mariae* (2002).

Glorious Mysteries

1. The Resurrection
2. The Ascension
3. The Descent of the Holy Spirit
4. The Assumption of Mary
5. The Coronation of the Blessed Virgin Mary

Passages of Marian Import in the New Testament

Gospel of Matthew
Chapters 1 and 2
Matthew 12:46–50
Matthew 13:53–58

Gospel of Mark
Mark 3:31–35
Mark 6:1–6

Gospel of Luke
Chapters 1 and 2
Luke 3:23
Luke 8:19–21
Luke 11:27–28

Gospel of John
John 1:13
John 2:1–11
John 6:42
John 8:41
John 19:25–27

Acts of the Apostles
Acts 1:14

Book of Revelation
Chapter 12

Galatians
Galatians 4:4

Marian Liturgical Celebrations

The following Marian celebrations are from the Universal Calendar of the Roman Rite:

January 1	Mary, Mother of God
February 2	The Presentation of Our Lord [with a Marian dimension, so also previously known as the Purification of Our Lady]
February 11	Our Lady of Lourdes
March 25	The Annunciation of Our Lord [with a Marian dimension, so also known as Lady Day]
May 13	Our Lady of Fatima
May 24	Mary, Help of Christians
May 31	The Visitation of the Blessed Virgin Mary
Moveable	The Immaculate Heart of Mary [Saturday following the Solemnity of the Sacred Heart of Jesus]
July 16	Our Lady of Mount Carmel
August 5	Dedication of the Basilica of St. Mary Major
August 15	The Assumption of the Blessed Virgin Mary
August 22	The Queenship of Mary
September 8	The Nativity of the Blessed Virgin Mary
September 12	The Most Holy Name of Mary
September 15	Our Lady of Sorrows

October 7	Our Lady of the Rosary
November 21	The Presentation of the Blessed Virgin Mary
December 8	The Immaculate Conception of the Blessed Virgin Mary
December 12	Our Lady of Guadalupe

NOTES

1. J. Neville Ward, *Five for Sorrow, Ten for Joy* (New York: Doubleday, 1975).

2. John Henry Newman, "Virgo Purissima" (May 3), *Prayers, Verses, and Devotions* [hereafter, *PVD*] (San Francisco: Ignatius Press, 1989), 115.

3. John Henry Newman, *Certain Difficulties Felt by Anglicans in Catholic Teaching* [hereafter, *Diff.*] (New York: Longmans, Green, and Co., 1907), vol. II, 85.

4. John Henry Newman, "Rosa Mystica" (May 7), *Meditations and Devotions* [hereafter, *MD*] (New York: Longmans, Green, and Co., 1907), 127.

5. John Henry Newman, "The Annunciation: The Honour Due to the Blessed Virgin," his first sermon preached on Our Lady (March 25, 1831), in *Mary: The Virgin Mary in the Life and Writings of John Henry Newman*, ed. Philip Boyce (Grand Rapids, MI: William B. Eerdmans Publishing Co., 2001), 105–28.

6. John Henry Newman, "On the Fitness of the Glories of Mary" (Discourse XVIII), *Discourses Addressed to Mixed Congregations* [hereafter, *Mix.*] (New York: Longmans, Green, and Co., 1909), 368–69.

7. "Mater Christi" (May 15), *PVD*, 145–46.

8. From Sermon 169, in Donald X. Burt, OSA, *Day by Day with Saint Augustine* (Collegeville, MN: Liturgical Press, 2006), 253.

9. Bernard of Clairvaux, from the homily "In Praise of the Virgin Mother," *Office of Readings*, December 20.

10. "Regina Angelorum" (May 10), *PVD*, 134.

11. "Sancta Maria" (May 9), *PVD*, 132–33.

12. "Domus Aurea" (May 6), *PVD*, 122.

13. "A Short Service for Rosary Sunday," *MD*, 261–62.

14. *Diff.*, vol. II, 82–83.

15. *Diff.*, vol. II, 47.

16. John Henry Newman, "The Reverence Due to the Virgin Mary," *Parochial and Plain Sermons* [hereafter, *PPS*] (New York: Longmans, Green, and Co., 1908), vol. 2, 128–29.

17. *Diff.*, vol. II, 32.

18. Fulton J. Sheen, *Treasure in Clay* (Garden City, NY: Doubleday, 1980), 156.

19. Fulton J. Sheen, *Life of Christ* (New York: McGraw-Hill, 1958), 14.

20. Ibid., 5.

21. "Religious Joy," *PPS*, vol. 8, 251–52.

22. Augustine, *De Sancta Virginitate*, 3.

23. *Diff.*, vol. II, 55–56.

24. "Consolatrix Afflictorum" (May 21), *PVD*, 158–59.

25. Thomas C. Oden, ed., *Luke in Ancient Christian Commentary on Scripture* (Downers Grove, IL: InterVarsity Press, 2003), 55.

26. "The Glories of Mary for the Sake of Her Son" (Discourse XVII), *Mix.*, 346–48.

27. "On the Teaching of the Greek Church about the Blessed Virgin," *Diff.*, vol. 2, 153–64.

28. Paul VI, Address at Nazareth (January 5, 1964), *Office of Readings*, Holy Family Sunday.

29. Pius XII, Allocution to Newlyweds (March 11, 1942).

30. "On the Fitness of the Glories of Mary" (Discourse XVIII), *Mix.*, 362.

31. *Diff.*, vol. II, 72–73.

32. "Sedes Sapientiae" (May 12), *PVD*, 139.

33. Based on *The Way of the Cross according to the Method of St. Alphonsus Liguori* (Rockford, IL: TAN Books, 1987), 11.

34. Ibid.

35. "The Fourth Station," *PVD*, 223–24.

36. *Diff.*, vol. II, 84.

37. "Vas Insigne Devotionis" (May 18), *PVD*, 152–53.

38. Benedict XVI, *Regina Caeli* Address (May 9, 2010).

39. "May the Month of Joy" (May 2), *PVD*, 113–14.

40. "Virgo Prudentissima" (May 22), *PVD*, 160–61.

41. John Paul II, Wednesday Audience Address (January 25, 1997).

42. "Sancta Dei Genitrix" (May 24), *PVD*, 164–65.

43. John Henry Newman, *Apologia pro Vita Sua* (New York: Longmans, Green, and Co., 1908), 239.

44. "Mater Intemerata" (May 25), *PVD*, 166–67.

45. "Rosa Mystica" (May 26), *PVD*, 168–69.

46. "Mater Intemerata" (May 25), *PVD*, 167.

47. "Turris Davidica" (May 27), *PVD*, 170–71.

48. "Vas Honorabile" (May 19), *PVD*, 154–55.

49. John Henry Newman, "The Theory of Developments in Religious Doctrine" (Sermon XV), *Oxford University Sermons* (New York: Longmans, Green and Co., 1909), 312–13.

50. "Auxilium Christianorum" (May 29), *PVD*, 174–75.

51. Thomas Aquinas, *Summa Theologiae*, III, Q. 43, Art. 1 (trans. by the Fathers of the English Dominican Province, 1948, accessed at sacred-texts.com).

52. *Diff.*, vol. II, 21.

53. Ibid., 73.

54. "On the Glories of Mary" (Discourse XVII), *Mix.*, 344.

55. *Summa Theologiae*, III, Q. 43, Art. 1.

56. Ibid.

57. "Miracles No Remedy for Unbelief," *PPS*, 86–87.

58. John Henry Newman, *Lectures on the Present Position of Catholics in England* (New York: Longmans, Green, and Co., 1908), 305.

59. *Diff.*, vol. II, 26.

60. Benedict XVI, *Regina Caeli* Address (May 9, 2010).

61. "Rosa Mystica" (May 7), *PVD*, 126–27.